FIRST EDITION

THE
TORAH ZONE
AN
Anthology of Articles

By Lew White

Selected articles from the website
www.fossilizedcustoms.com
In book form

Who founded Christianity?
It wasn't who you might think!
Why has it been so successful?
Becoming the state religion of Rome perhaps?
Why does this religion have a Greek name?
Odd thing, isn't it?
What is the Creator's religion?
It's been right under your nose all along!

THE
TORAH ZONE
AN
Anthology of Articles

By Lew White

First Edition
C.E. 2006
ISBN: 0-9585045-1-2
Distributed by:

Strawberry Islands Messianic Publishing

2303 Watterson Trail, Louisville, KY 40299
For ordering information call:
502-261-9833
FAX: 502-297-9854
www.fossilizedcustoms.com

This book is dedicated to the bride of Yahuah

YISRA'EL

A reminder . . .

You are mortal, so one day you will face the end of your physical existence.
Live each moment serving the One that created you, and follow His Torah.
Enter into the eternal Covenant by being immersed in the Name of Yahushua.

Enter the Torah Zone.

"Though ㄱYㄱㄥ gave you bread of adversity and water of affliction, your Teacher shall no longer be hidden, but your eyes will see your Teacher, and your ears hear a word behind you, saying, 'this is the Way, walk in it,' whenever you turn to the right, or when ever you turn to the left." Yesha Yahu 30:20,21

HOW MUST WE LIVE?

Our Creator designed us to live according to His instructions, which is called "TORAH" in Hebrew. We can be easily diverted and deceived by traditions, men's teachings, or our own opinions and drives, but in the final analysis there is a **standard of perfection** which we will all one day have to concede has been the original plan. "Faith" and "obedience" are comparable to the two sides of the same coin. If we have **belief** without the "works" that prove it, then we are living a lie - either our own or someone else's. We have a Messiah, Yahushua L'Natsarith, Who has come to bring us His life, and enable us to find the Truth, and obey it through His Spirit which is given to those who obey Him (Acts 5:32).

How we live is a mixture of how we were molded, and what we have chosen to accept or reject. The Hebraic concept of how we live is called "halakah", from the word **halak**, referring to our "walk". The "way" or "path" on which we do this "walking" is either *the narrow path of light* (as Torah directs us in its teachings/directions), or *the broad road of darkness* that follows no directions from Torah. This road leads to death (the eternal kind). The **Torah** is our map, to direct us into "paths of righteousness" which YHWH guides us into "for His Name's sake". All who call on His true Name must depart from all unrighteousness, or it brings shame upon His Name.

How do **_you_** live? Most of us are raised in a denomination or mold, called "a **religion**". These may be all **_about_** the Messiah. But, are any of them the Messiah's religion?
1 Yn 2:6 says,
"The one who says he stays in Him ought _himself_ _also_ to walk, even _as_ He walked."
It's **_how_** we walk (our halakah) that reveals the truth about whether our "religion" is **_His_** religion, or is just "about" Him. One is the path of light, guided by the **Torah**, and the other is

designed by traditions of men to win the approval of men —
seminary-trained, but flawed in their walk, having exchanged
the Commandments of YHWH for the _traditions_ of men.
Unless your conscience is completely numbed by listening to
the intoxicating excuses and deceiving teachings, you know
that most have fulfilled the prophecy that there would be an
"apostasy", or _falling-away_ from the Torah, the true faith.
What is right, or righteous, can only be determined or defined
by the Torah — not the masquerading messengers of light
who fill our heads with traditional lies that have no basis in
Scripture.   Test everything, especially the excuses you are
taught, and ask for the _clear, Scriptural_ foundation they base
their teachings upon.   If we are taught that we no longer
have to obey a Commandment, there had better be clear
Scriptural verses to show this to be true.   A good place to
start investigating would be to study the 4th Commandment,
concerning the "Shabbath", which commands us to rest on
the 7th day of each week — in commemoration of Creation
week.   Has this Commandment been annulled by ᐱY𐤀𐤆, or
men?

> _"Kepha and the other apostles replied:_
> _'We must obey_ ᐱY𐤀𐤆 _rather than men!'"_ Acts 5:29

Through the experience of just being alive and living
among other people like myself, I know that the vast majority
are simply blundering through, hoping to discover something
worthwhile to put their trust in.   We often ask _"What is your
religion?"_ of one another.   We get all kinds of answers to this,
but what if we stop asking **each other** that question, and ask
our Creator _"What is _Your_ religion?"_   He won't answer the
question the way we normally do, because He KNOWS the
right answer.   We only hope to know it.   This book will at
least teach you what the right answer is, and hopefully much
more.   If you are blessed enough to ever stand before the
Throne of the Universe, and He asks you _"What is your religion?"_, you can answer it correctly because you know it will
have to match HIS answer to that same question.   The answer is:

THE TORAH OF YAHUAH

"**TORAH**" is the Hebrew word for teaching, or instruction;
Yahuah has used it throughout His revealed Word as the pat-

tern all mankind is to live by. The articles in this book reflect the opposite opinion of what men generally choose to accept. They usually prefer to pick and choose what they like from Scripture, and leave out what they don't care for. Picture for a moment that you have died, and are awakened in the resurrection. You are standing before your Maker, Who is smiling at you. Moments pass, and you hear nothing; then, suddenly, from behind in the distance, a voice cries out in accusation of you!

"This human had the nerve to attempt to obey Your Commandments (Torah), *and repeatedly tried to teach others to also obey them! This being is a LEGALIST!"*

Can you imagine, given the circumstances, for anything *better* to be said of you? Yet, in *this* deceived world, there are few who seem to comprehend the level of deception taking place. These articles attempt to answer questions from the perspective of what Yahuah revealed to us in His Word. Whether we like the Scriptural opinion or not reveals one important thing: we either have the mind of Mashiach, or we don't. If we are in agreement with Him, then He has changed our hearts so that we love to obey. When we obey His Torah, we have fellowship with Him, and with those He has chosen. If we do not obey, and yet claim to have fellowship with Yahuah (know Him), then we are deceiving ourselves.

"We know that we have come to know Him if we obey His Commands. The man who says, 'I know Him,' but does not do what He commands is a liar, and the truth is not in him. But if anyone obeys His Word, Yahuah's love is truly made complete in him. This is how we know we are in Him: whoever claims to live in Him must walk as Yahushua did." 1 John / Yahuchanon 2:3-6

BEGIN ARTICLES:

THE NAME OF THE CREATOR OF THE UNIVERSE

Here are some ideas on how it originally looked, and may have sounded. It means: "I WAS, I AM, I WILL BE": existence in all three tenses: ETERNAL BEING.

"I will be there" is one way of stating the meaning, however this is a *unique* Hebrew word containing all three

6

"tenses" of past, present, and future. This triple-tense is also seen in the phrase, "Who *is* and Who *was* and Who *is to come*, the Almighty", spoken by Yahushua of Natsarith, Rev. 1:8. His Name means He exists in all of time and space: OMNI-TEMPORALITY and OMNI-PRESENCE -- He's *there!* We're "finite", but the Creator is infinite. This Hebrew word is unique, in that it contains all three tenses; past, present, and future, so it makes some sense that it has three syllables, not two.

The word **YAHUDAH** (the tribe of Yisrael) is the doorway to the actual sound. On page 7 is shown the palaeo-Hebrew script, which is the way the Name of YAHUAH physically appeared *as He wrote His personal Name in the stone tablets at Sinai with his own finger*. It is read from right-to-left. The letters are YOD, HAY, WAW, HAY. Our letter, "W" is a new letter, and is really what it is called: a "double-U" (UU). There's actually no letter in Hebrew that matches it better than our letter, "U" - (there's not a letter "W" in Hebrew). At the bottom of the illustration, you see the Name of YAHUSHUA, which is the real Name which most people have been taught is "JESUS". In the center is the word "YAHUDAH", which serves as a litmus test for how to really pronounce the Name -- it contains all four letters of the Name, but has the letter "DALET" (D) inserted just before the last letter.

"Whenever I said, 'Let me not mention Him, nor speak in His Name again,' it was in my heart like a burning fire shut up in my bones. And I became weary of holding it back, and was helpless." YIRMEYAHU 20:9

This is what the Encyclopedia Americana (1945 Edition) says under the topic "GOD":

"**GOD** *(god)* Common Teutonic word for personal object of religious worship, formerly applicable to super-human beings of heathen myth; on conversion of Teutonic races to Christianity, term was applied to Supreme Being." We respect everyone's attempts to pronounce the personal Name. The personal Name of our Creator as revealed at least 6,823 times in the TaNaKh is spelled:

YOD-HAY-WAW-HAY

Some of us prefer the literal sound of the letters as they appear comparatively in other Hebrew words, and the closest

(HEBREW READS RIGHT-TO-LEFT)

HAY   WAW   HAY   YOD

" ya - HOO - ah "

THESE SAME FOUR LETTERS ARE IN ANOTHER WORD:

THIS IS " YAHUDAH", HAVING THE ADDED LETTER "DALET":

DALET

IF WE ARE SAYING " YAHUDAH " CORRECTLY,

WE MUST HAVE " ya - HOO - ah " RIGHT ALSO!

THIS IS THE PALAEO-HEBREW FOR " YAHUSHUA ":

AYIN   SHIN

word using the identical letters in the same order as the Name happens to be: YAHUDAH (the fourth son of Leah, and the name of the tribe / family from which springs all those who today call themselves "Jews".

This man's name is spelled, in Hebrew:

YOD-HAY-WAW-DALETH-HAY

Notice the underlined letters, and imagine the sound of this word without the sound of the "D":

YOD-HAY-WAW-DALETH-HAY

Clement of Alexandria trans-lettered the Name from Hebrew into Greek using the following: IAOUE

The limitations of electronic text communications (like the internet) cause us to use the Latin letters "YHWH" as an abbreviated form for the four letters of yod (Y), hay (H), waw (W), hay (H). YaHUaH is another way of rendering the four letters, and probably more accurate, since there is no "W" in Hebrew - it's really simply a "U" (or an "O"). The appearance of the original Hebrew can best be used here in the form of a picture, and if viewed on the internet, most everyone would be looking at nonsense without the appropriate font installed on their system.

The Hebrew words adonai, elohim, eloi, eloah, and others are pronouns as you know. Many of us feel it is wrong to substitute formerly Pagan terms or names for Father YHWH, of course (like GOD). I've never found any Scriptures using the term "haShem" to replace the Name YHWH, yet we know it's in common use among many Messianics and orthodox Yahudim today. There's no letter "V" in older Hebrew, but modern Hebrew uses such a letter (since the 17th century). "Jehovah" is a hybrid mongrelization of the Tetragrammaton YHWH - changed to JHVH, then the vowels of "adonai" are crammed in, to "cue" the reader to not pronounce the Name, but instead say "adonai".

THE USE OF "HA-SHEM"

"Hashem" is used in sentences throughout the Scriptures, however it is not used as a substitution for the Name. If I write a sentence and say "the name" in it, you would expect me to also use the name these words refer to; and Scripture certainly does this. The Orthodox Yahudim enforced the human custom of saying "hashem" *in place of* the actual Name Yahuah when reading the Scriptures aloud, however there is not a single scrap of inspired Scripture to support this tradition, only Talmud, which is the written form of everything Yahushua found to be the greatest problem with the teachers of Yisrael long ago -- the leavening, or puffing-up, with men's traditions (traditions of the fathers).

Yahuchanon 17 clearly shows that Yahushua revealed the Father's Name to those whom He had given to Him out of the world, and said that He would reveal it again. "Hashem" is not it. The Orthodox Yahudim know the Name, but don't use it out of misguided respect and human tradition -- but they definitely know that "hashem" is not the Name. There are plenty of weird ideas on the internet, and people who have not thoroughly studied can draw some faulty conclusions.

Something tells me that calling on the words "hashem" won't quite make the grade, and this is far from what Yahuah intended.

EL SHADDAI

Some teach that the patriarchs only knew Yahuah by the term "El Shaddai" -- due to the translation of Exodus 6:3 which commonly reads: "And I appeared unto Abraham, unto Isaac, and unto Jacob, by ("the Name of" are added words) God Almighty (El Shaddai), but by My Name JEHO-VAH* was I not known to them." Ex. 6:3 KJV Being known as "El Shaddai" conveys the meaning of "Elohim Almighty", yes, but it is not a proper noun - it is a description of what He is. Yahuah is not saying this was known to them as a NAME, but that He was KNOWN to them as being El Shaddai, the all-mighty Elohim. The translations miss a simple fact concerning this text: it's a question! Here is a better rendering of what Yahuah actually meant to say:

"And I appeared to Abraham, to Yitzchak, and to Ya'akob, as El Shaddai; and by My Name YHWH, WAS I NOT KNOWN TO THEM?" Exodus 6:3 . . . *IT'S A QUESTION.*

The Scriptures we distribute corrects this text to read properly. If you check to see if Abraham used the proper Name, YHWH, you'll see that he did! So did all the other patriarchs. So, if we read these men's own quoted words, seeing they pronounced it aloud, then the common translations of Ex. 6:3 convey an incorrect message to people.

Exodus 6:3 is a *QUESTION*, making the meaning of the sentence different from what most have been led to understand. Examining the conversations with these men it is easy to see they knew the Name. Men began to call on His Name very early, as we see at Genesis 4:26.

Hebrew has many similarities to our language, and in fact there are a large percentage of common English words that derive from Hebrew roots. The Hebrew root "AB" as we see in the name "ABRAM" or "ABRAHAM" is two letters (AB = alef + beth). ABBA equates to the Latin word for "PATER", and this PATER has become the English word FATHER.

The Hebrew letters PE and FE are both represented with a single letter, PE. So a single Hebrew letter can have more

---

* IT'S VERY TRUE, HE WAS <u>DEFINITELY</u> NOT KNOWN TO THEM AS 'JEHOVAH' . . . UNTIL 1611

than one sound, just as our English letters can, depending on the word they are used in.

There is no letter "V" in the ancient Hebrew, but because Hebrew is a "living language", corruptions (changes) have occurred, so the modern Hebrew does have a letter sounding like a "V".

About the word ABBA; it's not a name, but a pronoun, just as FATHER isn't a name. It's like the word MOTHER; it's not a name. The Hebrew word for MOTHER is EMMA, which later became the Latin MATER, often shortened to "MA" by the hillbilly set.

YHWH refers to His "NAME" often in Scripture, and it's always associated with the same word: **Y**od-**H**ay-**W**aw-**H**ay. The "W" should be thought of as our letter "U", as we know the letter is called a "double—U".

Yahushua revealed the FATHER (and His Name) to His Talmidim, since Israel had not generally experienced YHWH as FATHER, but more often as El Shaddai. The translators of most editions of Scripture missed a subtle thing at Exodus 6:3. YHWH did not say His "NAME" was ever considered to be El Shaddai, but that He appeared to them "<u>as</u>" Elohim Al-mighty (El, Elah, Elohim, & Eloah are all pronouns, not names). Now that you know the Name of the Creator, allow me to share the Covenant of Yahuah - an *eternal* Covenant made between the **Maker** of Heaven and Earth, and **Israel**:

"And Elohim spoke all these words:

(FIRST):
'I am ꓤY∃Z *your Elohim, Who brought you out of Mits-rayim, out of the house of slavery.*
You shall have no other mighty ones against My face.

(SECOND):
You do not make for yourself an idol in the form of any-thing in heaven above or on the earth beneath or in the waters below. You do not bow down to them or worship them; for I, ꓤY∃Z *your Elohim, am a jealous El, punish-ing the children for the sin of the fathers to the third and fourth generation of those who hate Me, but showing kindness to thousands, to those who love Me and keep*

My Commands.

(THIRD):
You shall not bring the name of the 𐤉𐤄𐤅𐤄 your Elohim to naught, for 𐤉𐤄𐤅𐤄 does not leave the one unpunished who bring His Name to naught.

(FOURTH):
Remember the Sabbath day, to set it apart. Six days you labor and do all your work, but the seventh day is a Sabbath of 𐤉𐤄𐤅𐤄 your Elohim. On it you shall not do any work, neither you, nor your son or daughter, nor your manservant or maidservant, nor your animals, nor the alien within your gates. For in six days 𐤉𐤄𐤅𐤄 made the heavens and the earth, the sea, and all that is in them, but he rested on the seventh day. Therefore 𐤉𐤄𐤅𐤄 blessed the Sabbath day and set it apart.

(FIFTH):
Honor your father and your mother, so that your days are prolonged upon the soil which 𐤉𐤄𐤅𐤄 your Elohim is giving you.

(SIXTH):
You do not murder.

(SEVENTH):
You do not adulterate.

(EIGHTH):
You do not steal.

(NINTH):
You do not give false testimony against your neighbor.

(TENTH):
You do not covet your neighbor's house. You do not covet your neighbor's wife, or his manservant or maidservant, his ox or donkey, or anything that belongs to your neighbor. "   Ex 20:1-17

JESUIT INFLUENCES

The Jesuits (Society of Jesus) designed the Roman calendar we use, modeled on the previous Pagan Julian calendar. They also use "GREEK" to explain our English transliteration for the Name above-all-names.   Most are taught that the

Name "JESUS" is a *translation*. If this were so, then it could be "translated" into some meaning into English, Greek, Latin, or Hebrew, no? No one can "translate" it back to Hebrew. To "translate" means to convey the MEANING of a word, not its SOUND. The "sound" of a word taken into another language is a *TRANSLITERATION*. All scholars know that Yahushua never heard anyone say "Jesus" to Him 2000 years ago. It wasn't even invented until around 1530 CE, so how could anyone get "saved" in the name "Jesus" before it was invented? To try to make it mean something in Greek, the ending "sus" definitely refers to Zeus, as it does in many other Greek names such as Tarsus, Pegasus, Dionysus, and Parnassus. So, in Greek, the Name "JESUS" can mean "hail Zeus", or "son of Zeus". It means nothing in Hebrew, the language it supposedly came from! But, if you force it to mean anything, the closest it could come to any Hebrew word is "hey-horse", because "soos" is Hebrew for "horse". The name Yeshua can mean "help" or "save", but the true Name "YAHUSHUA" above means "YAH is our salvation". There is more to discover concerning the moniker "YESHU" (or JESCHU), which will be covered under another article in this book on "transliteration". The Yahudim have their own privately-kept secret regarding the meaning of some versions of Yahushua's Name: "Yeshu" is an acronym, where the letters stand for the words of this sentence: "may his name be blotted out!"

The association with Zeus in the "sus" ending is possibly an intended distortion, made by Pagan copyists of long ago. Zeus was sometimes depicted as a HORSE-MAN, or "centaur". The old Babylonian /Egyptian signs of the Zodiac/ Zoo beasts in the skies included a centaur holding a bow and arrow, called Sagittarius - this is really Nimrod, the mighty hunter. He was known as Orion the hunter also. Satan (shatan) masquerades, changes, distorts, and misleads. Even "satan" came across rather close to its original: shatan. And, like they say, the translators managed to get the name for the Yerushaliyim garbage dump correct also; but they just couldn't get the Name above all names right . . . . .

Why do most use the transliteration YAHWEH? Not to be critical, but ultimately this is because the *Jewish Encyclopedia* endorses this pronunciation. Remember, our brothers in

Rabbinical Judaism subscribe to the teachings of the TAL-MUD, and this written collection of human traditions _prohibits_ the utterance of the Name. The orthodox Yahudim (Jews) will let the information only go so far; "YAHWEH" is as close as they want anyone to really get. This is only my opinion, and I can be incorrect; but reason through it yourself. Do you really think they want anyone to be able to utter the Name? The doorway to the Name is the word YAHUDAH -- just remove the "D", and you have the closest probable sound of the Name. Look at the letters of YAHUDAH & YAHUAH:

Yod-**H**ay-**W**aw-**D**alet-Hay   **Y**od-**H**ay-**W**aw-**H**ay

The word YAHU<u>D</u>AH is the doorway to the actual sound!
(Take away the "D", and you have it).

The _translation_ of any word or phrase is to carry-across a meaning or interpretation from one language to another. Not **sounds**, but **thoughts** and **ideas** are transferred. What would otherwise be gibberish or confusion is explained and rendered understandable when the sound from one language is equated with a similar idea or concept in another. It matters not if the sound is written or spoken; the objective of **translating** a word is to convey or transfer the **meaning** of the word or concept, not the sound of it.

To **transliterate** a word from one language to another involves "trans-lettering" -- to take each corresponding letter from the original language and use the closest sounding letters in the target alphabet to duplicate the **exact sound** of the word. The meaning of the word is <u>not</u> <u>involved</u> in this transliteration process.

With this in mind, the name JESUS cannot fit into the idea of being a translation, since to do this it would have to have a meaning in the original language, then maintain that same meaning in the target language. Yahshua (or Yahushua, Y'shua) means "Yah is our salvation". Since it has been claimed (and defended by Jesuits for centuries) to be a translation into the Greek, the subsequently the Latin languages, it would be necessary to maintain some meaning in both languages that equivilates the meaning of "<u>Yah</u> <u>is</u> <u>our</u> <u>salvation</u>". Since this is not the case, the word JESUS is some sort of total replacement device, probably used in order to appeal to the hearers of the name. The Greeks' ambition was obviously to maintain the sound of some previously familiar name -- and since "koine" Greek was the language of the common people, the name Zeus was a natural choice to use. In some places in the former Soviet Union, the name JESUS is spelled JE-ZUS, having come directly from the koine Greek. The excuses used by the Jesuits to explain the name JESUS fall apart when the difference between "translate" and "transliterate" are explained.

The Name of our Messiah in the received Greek is written: IESOU and IESOUS. The ending "S" is added because the Greek language requires male names to end in s. How much tampering was done to the Name as it went into Greek? Apparently quite a bit - it sounds more like the Greeks simply inserted their former Pagan deity's name where it suited them.

The book *Come Out Of Her My People* shows how several ancient languages worshipped false deities under the names ESUS, ISIS, HESUS, and others. "BARUCH HABA BASHEM YAHUAH" is the *transliteration* of a Hebrew phrase, and the translation or meaning is: ***"Blessed is the one who comes in the Name of YHWH."*** Yahushua quoted these words from Psalm 118:26. This same text was called out by the crowds when Yahushua rode the colt into the city as they laid palm branches on the ground before Him, making the Pharisees and Sadducees become quite agitated (because they heard the common people using the Personal Name of YHWH). Knowing that the Name had been a point of stumbling, and was prohibited from being spoken aloud under penalty of stoning to death by human tradition, Yahushua prophetically declared, ***"For I say to you, from now on you shall not see Me until you say, 'BLESSED IS HE WHO COMES IN THE NAME OF YHWH!'"*** (See Mt. 23:39. The Natsarim (watchmen, branches) are saying it now, at the end of the times of the Gentiles. The key of knowledge is the personal Name, removed by most translators, and replaced by the capital letters LORD in the text (see any good translation's Preface for more on this human traditon). The Name is what we must be immersed in, but this vital information has been withheld from the "sheeple". Individually, we each must "overcome" the obstacles like this through personal study. References: Mt. 21:9, Mt. 23:39, Mk. 11:9, Lk. 13:35, Jn. 12:13

The following is from an Email sent by a gentleman named Douglas representing UCG (a denomination). He was presented with the initial evidence that the Name traditionally used is flawed, and that the true Name should be taught. His responses spring from boiler-plate answers baked in seminaries. I was asked to comment on his responses, so this is the way it went:

Douglas wrote: "Thank you for your letter, with your questions regarding the name of Jesus. You asked about the letter "J" in Christ's day. Our Roman alphabet (with the letter "J") was in common use at that time, as Judea was a province of the Roman Empire."

Lew's response: This is simply a statement that is not true, although Douglas may believe it sincerely. A good encyclopedia will reveal the truth about this in two ways; the article under the letter "J" will show its late development, stemming from the Greek letter iota (the English letter I). The other article to check carefully is "ALPHABET". It will clearly show there is no letter "J" in any language until the early 16th century. We use Latin letters, however there was no letter "J" in the Latin alphabet until the early 16th century, and neither did it exist in any other language before that time. So, the claim that "Judea" was in use 2000 years ago is like believing that General Sherman of the Civil War era used Sherman tanks . . . no, let's not do that either; it makes my brain hurt. In reality the Romans spelled the land of Israel "Ioudia" -- (see the chronology at http://www.argyrosargyrou.fsnet.co.uk/myths/bible/ChronologyD.htm).

Douglas wrote: "However, many educated Jews and Romans also spoke Greek, with its slightly different alphabet. The New Testament, as you may realize, was written mostly in Greek (with some Aramaic). The Greek alphabet, with 24 letters, has no exact equivalent to the Roman "J." The closest may be "iota," most similar to our letter I."

Lew's response: Actually, the "inspired Greek N.T." is a myth being exposed more everyday. There are a half dozen existent texts of MattithYahu, and an early pre-Nicene "Church father" stating that MattithYahu wrote in the original Hebrew, not even Aramaic. Another oddity is that there has been no discovery of any Aramaic in the land they call

"Palestine" during the Roman occupation. Modern scholarship admits the numerous idioms within the received Greek transmission, and they are strong indicators of a Hebrew original for all the original autographs. Yahushua and most of His talmidim were not likely bi-lingual, although we know Shaul spoke several languages. The mother tongue of all the early talmidim was Hebrew, and if they even spoke another language such as Greek it certainly would not be likely for them to write their letters in their second language.

Douglas wrote: "The Hebrew alphabet (the language of the Old Testament) has 22 letters, and once again, there is no direct counterpart to our "J," although "yod" may be the closest (it is generally equated to "Y")."

Lew's response: Indeed this is true, so we can forego discussing the intermediary Greek hopefully. Or not . . . . .

Douglas wrote: "The name given to Joseph and Mary for their son would have been the name anglicized as "Joshua" from the Hebrew, and "Jesus" from the Greek. They are essentially the same name, meaning "YHWH is salvation." "YHWH" is one of the most common names for God in the Old Testament Hebrew, but since the Jews felt it was too holy a name to pronounce, the vowel points were lost over time. Some render it as "Jehovah," but this is generally acknowledged as incorrect, and there is really no way to know now how it should have been pronounced. The word "LORD" (with capital letters in many English versions) in the Old Testament is from "YHWH." It generally means something like "the Eternal One.""

Lew's response: Yahuah is the only personal Name given for our Creator, **Y**od-**H**ay-**W**aw-**H**ay, and means existence in all 3 tenses, past-present-future. This is His "memorial Name" (Shemoth 3:14,15), used at least 6,823 times between Bereshith and Malachi. "LORD" is an English word, and means BAAL, and is not only the abomination it appears to be, but is also against the literal intention of the 3rd Commandment (look up "Baal" in Websters dictionary). The *NIV* preface admits it to be a "device", *used to stand in the place of the true Name*, obliterating it, probably with the objective of placating the masses who would be offended to hear the true Name for whatever reason. "LORD" is a placebo, a concealment, and a substitution. The revealed true Name turned the world upside down, and it is happening again right now, before your eyes, in the latter rain.

Douglas wrote: "In Hebrews 4:8 (one of the verses to which you refer), the name is given as "Joshua" in the New King James Translation, but with a marginal reference that it could be rendered "Jesus." The context implies it should be translated "Joshua," but since the name came from Hebrew, it could have been translated either way. In Greek, it would be "Iesous" (the most direct transliteration to the Roman alphabet from the Greek)."

Lew's response: There's that Greek again. If we have the original Hebrew, we can toss the Greek transitional errors now. The Jesuits put great effort into destroying the Hebrew writing they found in libraries and private homes, so thoroughly that they also killed the people the documents were found with. They promote the myth of the inspired Greek N.T., and if there is a source for the promotion of the word "JESUS", it's the Jesuits, the "Society of Jesus".

Douglas wrote: "You are quite right to point out that Jesus came "in His Father's name." This powerfully indicated that He came by the Father's authority and to do His will (John 5:30; 17:2). Even today, a police officer might call out "Open the door, in the name of the law!" He doesn't mean that his name is "law," but that he has the authority and backing of the law behind him as a peace officer. The verse to which you refer (Psalm 68:4) mentions the name "YAH" is a shortened version of "YHWH" as the marginal reference in some Bibles states."

Lew's response: The standard "boiler plate" answer provided by seminary indoctrinated individuals concerning the word "authority" is well-stated above. Actually, the truth concerning Yahushua's Name being "YAH" is more literal than most would like to hear, because they have been exposed to traditional error so long that their minds are clouded with the "wine" (that keeps them asleep, drunk, or in a stupor). Many prophets not only spoke "in the Name" of YHWH, but openly pronounced it when they prophesied; and their own personal names were often based on the Name "YAH" as well. Yahushua (mistranslated "JOSHUA"), Yesha Yahu (mistranslated "ISAIAH"), Baruch Yah, ObadYah (Obadiah), to name but a few examples of this fact. The masses would prefer to use "generic" terms rather than the true, one Name, and this is not their fault - it's simple ignorance because of tradition. The prophet Yerme Yahu (mistranslated Jeremiah) tells us, *"My people will know My Name".* He further states at 23:27, *"They think the dreams they tell one another will make My people forget My Name, just as their fathers forgot My Name through BAAL (LORD)."*

Altering His Name in any way is as the sacrifice of Cain - we cannot make up our own method of worship nor call upon whatever name we feel we wish to call Him. "Well, isn't that special" -- is not what He is likely to say when we meet Him face-to-face. As teachers, we are held to a higher standard than to condone traditions that sound more like pretzel logic than anything else. Either His Name is Yahuah, or it's BAAL (LORD) -- and El Yahu (Elijah) could explain this best.
Yerme Yahu declared at 16:19, *"To you the nations will come from the ends of the Earth and say, 'our fathers have inherited nothing but falsehood, futility, and things of no profit.'"* Yesha Yahu (Isaiah) 28:15 says, *"We have made a lie our refuge, and falsehood our hiding place."* The *Name* of Yahuah is a strong tower of refuge, and those who are righteous run to it (Proverbs 18:10).

This is only a light encounter and far from a thorough examination of the Name, but the importance of being immersed into the true Name of Yahushua cannot be overly stressed. Do we want to relax in the thinking that the Jesuit-promoted word "Jesus" is good enough, or can we overcome the errors and accept the love of the true Name of the One who died for us and lives in us to guide us into all truth?
Praise YaHUaH - *hallelu Yah*

WHAT IS THE GOSPEL?

The true message is a secret.

The Hebrew word for "Gospel" is *BESORAH*. When the true Besorah is given, it will be accompanied by the special mention of a certain woman's deed recorded at Mt. 26:6-13. It is veiled to most by "another Gospel".

THE ENGLISH WORD "GOSPEL" AN ANALYSIS:

The word "Gospel" is Old English. It's really 2 words crammed together: GOD + SPEL. We have already seen that the Teutonic Celts worshipped the sun with the word "GOD", and it was a proper name; but for review here is that data again:This is what the Encylopedia Americana (1945 Edition) says under the topic "GOD":

"**GOD** (*god*) Common Teutonic word for personal object of religious worship, formerly applicable to super-human beings of heathen myth; on conversion of Teutonic races to Christianity, term was applied to Supreme Being."

The word "GOD" was used because it was already a familiar word to them, coming from the Greeks' translation for "Theos". The Greeks used THEOS instead of "Elohim", because they were already familiar with their old word also. The Greeks called Zeus "Theos", and their letter "theta" was originally a circle with a dot in the center, representing the sun running across the sky. They called all their deities by the title "Theos". Some scholars believe that using "GOD" and "THEOS" to refer to YHWH is the prophesied abomination of desolation. Pillars of Jealousy (steeples), Sun-day, calling Yahushua "Yeh-Zeus", Easter, and more yet to be exposed follow in that line of thought.

The second part of the word "Gospel", *SPEL*, is also Celtic in origin. It means incantation, speech, spiel, news, message, or report. It is the **spell** spoken to others. In 1948 CE, A. W. Tozer wrote the following words, underscoring how we can become swept up in mindless devotion by imitating others:
"Christian literature, to be accepted and approved by the evangelical leaders of our times, must follow very closely the same train of thought, a kind of 'party line' from which it is scarcely safe to depart. A half-century of this in America has made us smug and content. We imitate each other with slavish devotion and our most strenuous efforts are put forth to try to say the same thing that everyone around us is saying."

The true "Gospel" (BESORAH) is *virtually unknown* by most people on Earth today, yet collections to "spread" the "Gospel" are being donated to men who don't know what it is. It's all wasted, because like cancer researchers, they stumble in great darkness. The original followers of Yahushua carried its free message, but it died out (on the surface) with the last of the Nazarenes (Natsarim) and Ebionites before the 4th century. The Writings reveal that it is a SECRET, and a mystery, and will one day be revealed just before the end of men's kingdoms. It is directed only for the understanding of those whose names are written in the Scroll of Life, sealed with 7 seals. These are the BRIDE of Mashiach (Yisrael).

The wedding betrothal occurred at Sinai, when the children of Yisrael listened to the Voice of their *Groom*, and agreed to *obey* Him. Other "sheep" not of this fold (currently Gentiles) will *also* take the Name of the Groom. We'll discuss this in greater detail here. The word "*Gospel*" is one of many words we have inherited from dead translators that has taken on a kind of life of its own. Even encyclopedias admit that it is a bit "fuzzy". Scholars accept the term, but both what it is, and how the term came into use, are not clearly understood. The word's meaning and use is the result of our imitating each other for centuries, or our attempting to say the same thing everyone around us is saying. People who want to defend the altered names and other words they are conditioned to use by imitation sometimes will say, *"Well, I speak English, and not some foreign language."*

English is like a wide river with many other languages flowing into it. "Gospel" is Celtic. "Evangelical" is Greek (from euangelion, meaning message, or report). It became the Latin word evangelium. You can see the word "angel" in both, which simply means messenger (messages are carried by messengers). "Epistle" is Greek for letter. Many words we think of as English are really Celtic, Latin, Greek, French, Hebrew, or aboriginal tongues spoken by the natives of an area prior to English settlers. Rivers, states, and countries are often named by "foreign" terms. They're not "English", but our familiarity with them causes us to believe they are. When Rabbi Yahushua was in the synagogue (Mt. 11) and read from the TaNaKh, He read aloud in Hebrew the words of Yesha Yahu 61. He told them that this prophecy had been fulfilled in their ears! He announced the fulfillment of the prophecy of the awaited Mashiach, as His listeners comprehended. He proclaimed the "acceptable year of YHWH", known as the year of Jubilee (every 50th year, native-born Yahudim are to be freed, and land is to be returned to the heirs according to their tribes). He was also proclaiming the "Gospel": the announcement that the "Reign of YHWH" had come into their midst. If you read all of Yesha Yahu 61 & 62, you'll discover that it promises the day when the "Bridegroom" will rejoice over His BRIDE. At Mt. 11:5 where this passage of Yesha Yahu is being quoted, the word "Gospel" appears in our translation from the original Hebrew word BASAR (or BESORAH), meaning tidings, message, report, or news. You must know what the message is, to carry it to others. THE REIGN OF YHWH (Otherwise known as the "Kingdom of GOD"). A kingdom is a government.

How do we know it's a secret? *He told us it is:*
"And when He was alone, those about Him, with the 12, asked Him about the parable. And He said to them, 'To you it has been given to know the SECRET of the REIGN OF YHWH, but to those who are outside, all are done in parables, so that seeing they see but do not perceive, and hearing they hear but do not understand, lest they should turn (repent) and their sins be forgiven them'".
Mark 4:11,12   (He was quoting Yesha Yahu 6:9).

The "secret" or "mystery" is really the "Gospel" itself. At Romans 16:25:   "Now to Him who is able to establish you according to my (GOSPEL) and the preaching of Yahushua ha Mashiach, according to the revelation of the MYSTERY which has been kept SECRET for long ages past . . ." So, the "GOSPEL" isn't something new, but was first spoken to Abraham (see Gal. 3:8, Gen. 12:3). Abraham was called-out from among Pagans and Gentile practices, and was ultimately to become a blessing to the Gentiles because of his "fidelity" (faithfulness, emunah). Paul had to sternly warn the Gentiles who had converted at Galatia, and to those at Ephesus (4:17,18) he said: *"This I say therefore, and affirm together with YHWH, that YOU NO LONGER WALK AS THE GENTILES WALK, in the futility of their thinking, being darkened in their understanding, excluded from the Life of YHWH, BECAUSE OF THE IGNORANCE THAT IS IN THEM, because of the hardness of their heart."*

They were simply overwhelmed by the Pagan patterns of everyday living. When Paul stood before the Greek idolaters in Athens, he stood as Yonah had in Nineveh:
"Therefore having overlooked the times of ignorance,

YHWH is now declaring to men that all everywhere should REPENT, because He has fixed a day in which He will judge the world in righteousness through a Man whom He has appointed, having furnished PROOF to all men by raising Him from the dead." Acts 17.

The **Reign of Yahuah** will be, to most, like a trap spring-ing-shut, and catch the majority by complete surprise. They are in a Roman system, ignorant of the annual observances they are taught are "Jewish". Weekly Shabbat, Passover, Shabuoth (Pente-cost), Yom Teruah, Yom Kippur, and Sukkot (Tabernacles) all picture the **redemption** of YHWH's Bride, but they are kept from the knowledge of the plan, and what to watch for*. (For those unaware, Paul used to be "Sha'ul"). Paul explains it is a mystery to the Ephesians at 6:19: *"and pray on my behalf, that utterance may be given to me in the opening of my mouth, to make known with boldness the MYSTERY of the (GOSPEL) . . ."* (see also Eph. 3:3-9).

In Col. 1, Paul states his goal is *"That I might fully carry out the preaching of the Word of YHWH, the MYSTERY of which has been hidden from the past ages and genera-tions, but has now been manifested in His qodeshim (set-apart ones, saints) TO WHOM YHWH willed to make known what is the riches of the esteem of this SECRET among the Gentiles (the Torah written on your hearts) which is: MASHIACH IN YOU, expectancy of esteem, Whom we announce, WARNING every man and TEACH-ING every man in all WISDOM* (Torah, the Commandments), *in order to present every man perfect in Mashiach Ya-hushua . . ."* Shaul's reference to Mashiach <u>in</u> you indicates that the believer is ENABLED to LOVE the Torah, and thus obey it (YHWH's Word), because His "seed" (the Command-ments) came into the Nazarenes literally, fulfilling Yerme Yahu 31, implementing the New Covenant: *"'But this is the Covenant which I will make with the house of Yisrael after those days', declares YHWH, 'I will put my Torah within them, and on their HEART I will write it . . .'"* Again, at Ezek. 36:26,27: *"I will give you a new heart and put a new spirit in you; I will remove from you your heart of stone and give you a heart of flesh. And I will put My Spirit IN YOU, and move you to follow My decrees and be careful to keep My laws."* This prophecy is quoted at Heb.

* This is covered in a later article, beginning on page 174

10:16, and 2Cor. 3:3, and it first occurred at "Pente-cost" (the commanded convocation called "Shabuoth", which commemorates the giving of Torah at Sinai). Receiving the Torah is the "good seed", the Word of YHWH to walk in. Paul is quoted very often by today's preachers when they need to justify their "freedom" from the Commandments, making "sin" more of a state of the heart than a tangible, definable thing. Sin is definable, because 1 Yahuchanon 3:4 says: *"Everyone who sins breaks the Torah; in fact SIN IS TORAHLESSNESS."* (anti-nomia, lawlessness). Yahushua came to destroy the devil's work in us, and Yahuchanon goes on at 3:9 saying: *"No one who is born of YHWH will continue to sin, because YHWH's seed remains in him; he cannot go on sinning, because he has been born of YHWH. This is how we know who the children of YHWH are and who the children of the devil are: Anyone who does not do what is right is not a child of YHWH; nor is anyone who does not love his brother."*

2Pet. 3:15,16 discusses how this lawlessness was being propagated by DISTORTIONS OF PAUL'S WRITINGS: *"Our beloved brother Paul wrote to you according to the wisdom given him, as also in all his letters, speaking in them concerning these matters, IN WHICH SOME ARE HARD TO UNDERSTAND, WHICH THOSE WHO ARE UNTAUGHT AND UNSTABLE TWIST, as they do also the other Writings, to their own destruction. Therefore, dear friends, since you already know this, BE ON YOUR GUARD so that you may not be carried away by THE ERROR OF LAWLESS MEN and fall from your secure position."*

The "merchants" draw away your attention to the fact that Peter is calling Shaul's words "Scripture", but they cause you to overlook the serious warning of Peter talking about the very men you are listening to! Paul is always the one they quote to "prove" the Torah is no longer in force, yet here is Peter warning us of "falling" for that lie. (Paul is speaking of the "ceremonial" law coming to an end). The "Message", called the "Gospel", is very simple. The Writings are very clear about what it is, but listening with "lawless" ears, it is veiled to those who are perishing. Here it is from the mouth of our Creator Himself Who came to speak it to us: *"'The time has come, He said. 'The Kingdom of YHWH is near. Repent and believe the good news'"*. Mark 1:15. *"The Torah and Nebi'im* (Law, or Teachings, and prophets) *were proclaimed through Yahuchanon. Since that time, the good news of the Reign of YHWH is being preached, and everyone is forcing his way into it. It is easier for heaven and Earth to disappear than for the least stroke of a pen to drop out of the Torah."* (Luke 16:16,17). What "Gospel/ good news" have you been taught all your life? Commonly, it involves not being condemned for disobedience to the Torah. This is partly true, but it overlooks what the resurrection means to us, and what receiving Yahushua accomplishes, by His writing His Torah on our hearts! Sha'ul said to the Galatians, who were falling back into their old Pagan customs: "But even though we, or a messenger from the skies brings a message ("Gospel") to you besides what we announced to you, LET HIM BE ACCURSED." - Gal. 1:8.THE REAL MEANING

The real "Gospel" (message) is not the popular one. It is *"Repent, for the Reign of YHWH draws near."* Mt. 3:2, 4:17, Luke 16:16, Mark 1:15, Acts 8:12, etc.,.

In fact, ALL THE PARABLES describe it in great detail. The message of the Reign of YHWH is the subject matter of the parables, which veil its meaning from those not called. (Many are called, few chosen). *"I will open My mouth in a parable; I will utter dark sayings of old which we have heard and known, and our fathers have told us."* Ps. 78. You can praise the Living YHWH till you drop; but if you will not <u>obey</u> Him, your prayers and praise are an abomination, Pr. 15:8,9, 28:9, Yesha Yahu 1:15.

At 2Cor.4:3, Sha'ul states that he does not distort the "Word of YHWH", and says: *"Even if our besorah (Gospel) is veiled, it is veiled to THOSE WHO ARE PERISHING. The elohim (Shatan) of this age has blinded the minds of unbelievers, so they cannot see the Light of the besorah (Gospel) of the esteem of Mashiach, Who is the Image of YHWH."* At 2Cor. 2:15-17, Shaul speaks also of those perishing, and says something that might really open your eyes: *"Unlike so many, WE DO NOT PEDDLE THE WORD OF YHWH FOR PROFIT."* Remember, the "Word" of YHWH is His **Torah**, the 10 Commandments / Covenant that will <u>never</u> pass away until Heaven and Earth pass away. The "WE" would be the ones called the Nazarenes (more accurately "Natsarim"), who follow the Lamb where He leads us, into Truth. The "Gospel", or glad tidings, announcing that all men everywhere should REPENT (turn from sin, and obey Torah), is our commission: *"And these good tidings of the Kingdom shall be preached in the whole world for a testimony to all the nations; and then shall the end come."* Mt. 24:14. (Those who are perishing *do not understand the message*, and they are being plundered by false teachers who are profiting from the faith).

The first thing a person must do is be convicted of their sin against the Torah. Hearing first that their "sins are covered" doesn't emphasize repentance from sin, it sounds like they can live in their mind of the flesh, "believing". The adversary is also a "believer"; but obey? No way! The evidence that this is the true message (BESORAH) being taught throughout the world:

"While Yahushua was in Bethany in the home of a man known as Simon the Leper, a woman came to him with an alabaster jar of very expensive perfume, which she poured on his head as he was reclining at the table.

When the disciples saw this, they were indignant. "Why this waste?" they asked. "This perfume could have been sold at a high price and the money given to the poor."

Aware of this, Yahushua said to them, "Why are you bothering this woman? She has done a beautiful thing to me. The poor you will always have with you, but you will not always have me. When she poured this perfume on my body, she did it to prepare me for burial. I tell you the truth, wherever this gospel (BESORAH) is preached throughout the world, what she has done will also be told, in memory of her." Matt 26:6-13.

(THIS MUST BE THE TRUE BESORAH, BECAUSE IT IS ACCOMPANIED BY THE REPORT OF THE WOMAN'S ACTION, TOLD IN MEMORY OF HER).

Where is it written, that we will be punished for attempting to obey the Torah? Or, that we *"cannot possibly obey"* Torah? Your enemy wants you to ignore the Torah, just as he tricked the first woman. If we think she goofed over such a simple thing, then we should look at how we find ourselves in the very same situation. Shatan is a liar, and has many people following his masquerading messengers of lawlessness. "Legalism" and the accompanying criticisms cannot be found in the Writings anywhere. The merchant messengers will tell you "rest any day you like, just try to do it about every 7 days". They still "program" you to come to a Sun-day morning assembly, so you will be able to feel good about contributing to their wonderful "work". They are the "priests of **Baal**" (the **LORD**), wearing black. "The LORD's Day", Baal's Day, is Sun-day. Start obeying the 7th day Shabbat, and watch what they say to you. It's the sign of the Eternal Covenant, which we will see details of later. I picked the 7th day Shabbat to rest, and do it without fail. I'm "marked" now, with a *mark* called the *Sign* of the Eternal Covenant Ez. 20:12, Yesha Yahu 56:4-8, Ex. 31:12-17, Gen. 2:2, Heb. 4.

THE EVERLASTING COVENANT

The Everlasting Covenant establishes a new relationship between YHWH and mankind. It's the relationship of a Husband and His wife. It's metaphoric, or a figure of speech that draws an analogy. Like a *marriage*, there are two processes involved: betrothal and consummation. 50 days after leaving Egypt, representing the bondage of sin, the children of Yisrael (the chosen wife of the promise) were at Mount Sinai. This was the first "Shabuoth", now called "Pentecost". The elements found in the Everlasting Covenant correspond to Yahudim wedding traditions. YHWH refers to Yisrael as His "wife", because He has engaged in a formal betrothal. Sinai was this betrothal, and two written copies of the Torah (teachings, written in stone on front & back) were the marriage "ketuba". One for the Husband, and one for the wife. These were placed into a special container, called The Ark of the Covenant. The Husband chose His wife, Yisrael, to care for, provide for, and protect. The wife agreed to obey, forsaking all others. Two witnesses were called forth to hear the Covenant: shamayim (heavens, skies), and Eretz (Earth). They are the witnesses to the wife making her vows: *"All the words which YHWH has spoken we will do."* Ex. 24:3. At this point, the 70 elders of Yisrael (the Sanhedrin of the time) ate and drank with the Husband, Bridegroom, Creator, and Sovereign. The "wife" provided her contribution to the marriage covenant, a type of property brought by a bride to her husband at a marriage: the gold, silver, bronze, fabrics, oils, and precious stones for the construction of the ark and dwelling of the Husband among them. The terms of this formal Covenant (the written wedding agreement, or ketuba), were burned into stone with the finger of YHWH. The NAME of the Husband was taken by His wife; and so they (we) are called: YAHUDIM. This was corrupted to Judah, by translators, then Jude, and for the last several hundred years, it has been Jew. YHWH speaks of His Covenant (the marraige) without ceasing, reminding His wife of the marriage.

"For your Maker is your Husband ~ YHWH Shaddai is His Name" (Read all of Yesha Yahu 54, 55 & 56, and Ex. 31:13).

There is NO COVENANT of *any kind* with any other people of Earth than YHWH's wife, Yisra'el.

Not *"spiritual"** Israel; there's only ONE Israel, or body.

Gentiles must ENGRAFT (Romans 11, Ephesians 2:10-13).

GENTILES ALSO CALLED TO JOIN YISRAEL:

"Blessed is the man who does this, the man who holds it fast; who KEEPS THE SHABBATH without defiling it, and keeps his hand from doing any evil. LET NO FOREIGNER who has bound himself to YHWH say, 'YHWH will surely exclude me from His people'. And let not any eunuch complain, 'I am only a dry tree'. For this is what YHWH says: "To the eunuchs who keep My Shabbaths, who choose what pleases Me and hold fast to my Covenant ~ to them I will give within My Temple and its walls a memorial and a name better than sons and daughters; I will give them an everlasting name that will not be cut off. And FOREIGNERS who bind themselves to YHWH to serve Him, to love the Name of YHWH and to worship Him, ALL WHO KEEP THE SHABBATH without defiling it and who hold fast to My Covenant, these I will bring to My qodesh mountain and give them joy in My house of prayer . . . . For My house will be called a house of prayer for all nations.'" Yesha Yahu 56:2-7. Compare these words with Ephesians 2:8-13, all of chapter 3, and Acts 15. Notice there is a SECRET (mystery) of Elohim mentioned at Revelation 10:7. If a Gentile joins Israel, that being is no longer a Gentile (Eph. 2).

---

* Catholicism started the "spiritual Israel" nonsense as part of Replacement Theology

CHRISTIAN ~ the word's origin and use

The word is Greek, and has a formerly Pagan usage:

CHRESTOS MITHRAS - *pure, sacred, good, holy.*
(Roman meaning *was "good Mithras", or "holy Mithras")*
CHRIST HELIOS   (Mandaean)
CHREISTOS OSIRIS   (Alexandrian)

The question that begs to be asked is the following:

What would a bunch of Israelites that practice the Torah of YHWH and follow a Yahudi Messiah be doing with a Greek term used by Pagans as a label for themselves?

Look at the big picture, and keep an open mind for several options. Could there be a spiritual stronghold concerning this word? Knowing there is some relationship with the word **cretin**, what if the people of Antioch, at first, called the disciples **CRETINS** (retards, idiots)? Don't fall for the excuse, *"we speak English, not Hebrew"*. The word "crestos" (or kristos, chreistos) isn't English, it's Greek. If we follow the redemption plan of our Creator, we are members of the **commonwealth of Israel**; not a "Gentile", foreign nation. In fact, we are *no longer* Gentiles at all (Eph. 2:11-13). The main idea that people seem to be *steered away from* when words like this are examined closely is that the **original word** (the *Hebrew* word, MASHIACH) is not being brought to the table, but is typically kept from the discussion. Misdirection is used to convince the listener of supposed facts which are not true, and by simply saying the lie often enough, it will become familiar, and therefore comfortable. In this particular case, the premise is that the original word was this **Greek** word "Christos", since it is emphasized (by those with an agenda to preserve the error of tradition) that the disciples of Yahushua all spoke and wrote in Greek. We are expected to pay no mind that Greek is a **foreign language** to the people of Israel. It's a promotion of the Jesuits to believe that the Messiah and His students spoke to one another, and wrote everything down, in Greek. The truth is, Greek was a transitional language, or **translation**, of the original texts *originally written in Hebrew* (or the dialect of it, Syraic Aramaic). Remember, all the first "protestants" were Catholics, and they had already been indoctrinated with the

Jesuit teachings. What is practically unknown is the fact that *there were* "*Christians*" on Earth before Yahushua haMashiach was born - and they were Pagans.

The Greek word *"Christos"* (kristos) has come to mean anointed, and this corresponds to the Hebrew word Mashiach. What is not commonly known is that Osiris and Mithras were both called "Chreistos", which meant "GOOD". The word was adopted from gnostic Paganism:

The inscription "CHRESTOS" can be seen on a Mithras relief in the Vatican. During the time of Marcion, around 150 CE, Justin Martyr said that "Christians" were *"Chrestoi"*, or *"good men"*. Clement of Alexandria said *"all who believe in Christ are called "Chrestoi, that is 'good men'"*. Rome was the center of **Chrestos Mithras** worship, so the adaptation or revisionism to the new faith for this title should hardly be a huge mystery; but this information has been intentionally buried. The word "Christian" is only used 3 times in the received Greek texts; and if it were in fact what the disciples called themselves as a "sect", it would have seemed very foreign to not only them, but to everyone involved. Of course, *every Israelite* (and modern orthodox "Jew") believes in a "Mashiach" that is coming at some point. Many of them - in fact most - don't currently believe in the Mashiach portrayed by the "Christian" faith in any of its diverse denominations. However, if we *had* to adopt a Greek word for these practitioners of "Judaism" that related to them as believers in a *coming Mashiach*, then they too could be labeled "Christians". But, the word "Christian" is a very *non-specific* label when you consider that it doesn't specify *who* the Mashiach is. The true sect that followed Yahushua's teachings did use a term for themselves, and it was *NATSARIM* (Acts 24:5). Even the "Church father" Epiphanius wrote of the Natsarim, whom he called "heretics", because they observed the Commandments of YHWH and were indistinquishable from "Jews", except that they believed in the Mashiach.

In relation to the *Torah*, a Christian might well be considered to be retarded; but the actual word that means "retard" or "idiot" is derived from CHRISTIAN: *cretin!*
The *American Heritage Illustrated Encyclopedic Dictionary* tells us the etymology for the word *CRETIN*:

cre-tin (kre-tin, kret'n) *n.* **1.** One afflicted with Cretinism. **2.** A fool; an idiot. [French, *cretin,* from Swiss French, *crestin, CHRISTIAN,* hence human being (an idiot being nonetheless human).]

Cretinism is dwarfism and or retardation. Cretin is simply the word that is derived from the word CHRISTIAN, crestin. Greek is a corrupted, polluted language to begin with -- having many Pagan deities' names and titles associated with it. Since YHWH has told us that one day He would purify the lips of the peoples to call upon His Name and serve Him shoulder-to-shoulder (Zeph. 3:9), it's unlikely that the word "Christian" will be preserved after that purification takes place. Acts 24:5 states that the sect was called "*Natsarim*", or "branches/watchmen", not anointed ones. It was prophesied that we would be called "NATSARIM". Carefully study the text of Jer. 31. YermeYahu 31:6 used the word *NATSARIM* which is translated "watchmen", who will cry on "Mount Ephraim". The Gentiles, also known as "scattered Yisrael", is referred to in this chapter as "Ephraim". Those crying out to go up to YHWH are called *watchmen*, from the Hebrew word NATSARIM. The Greek has distorted quite a few things, but to believe that they were called both terms would surely be conflicted thinking. The *Natsarim* were very specific in their labeling of themselves, since their label referred to the One they were followers of, Yahushua of Natsarith. Chapter 31 of YermeYahu is also significant because it prophecies the renewed Covenant, which is quoted again in chapters 8 & 10 of the book of Hebrews.

All Israelites were, and are, waiting for the "Mashiach", the anointed One prophesied in Daniel. So by that logic it would be redundant to refer to themselves as a sect of what they all were, even if the label was translated into another tongue, like Greek. The translators simply wanted to separate themselves as far from the **Torah** and **Israel** as possible; and it was done by creating labeling that would permanently separate them, and keep "Gentiles" from ever joining the *commonwealth of Israel*, or even realizing that it was necessary.

Can you stand to hear more? Realize that "Greek" culture was a very powerful influence on the entire civilized world over a long period; "Alexandria" Egypt (named for Alexander, a famous Greek conqueror), became the center or hub of the cultural world. *Sophists*, orators who refined public speaking to an art, developed the "3-point" speech. They could convince their audiences of things they didn't even believe themselves! Clement and Origen, two "church fathers", promoted their Christian teaching from Alexandria. Everything taught became watered-down into "allegorical" meanings. In every way, words were used as powerful tools. Platonic philosophy steered their whole culture, and Plato is still quoted in modern seminaries! Mithraists, Neoplatonists, Pythagoreans, Therapists, and Magi were all contemporary cults. From Egypt arose the Hermetic religion of the worship of Osiris.

These religions produced the Pagan "fathers" that influenced modern Christianity (Cyprian, Augustine, Marcion, Eusebius, Ambrose, Epiphanius, etc.,) and they quoted from their former Pagan sources virtually constantly, merging what they had been with what they were becoming - a blended religion, with *Greek culture* as the dominant aspect. There already were "Christians" in Egypt, gnostic sun-worshippers who knelt before huge ankhs (crux ansatas). The Serapis-Isis cult used this symbol at Alexandria. When the Emperor Hadrian wrote from Alexandria, he said:
"Those who worship Serapis are Christians and those who call themselves bishops of Christ are vowed to Serapis".

Ancient Babylonian influences abounded then, and abound now, hidden in plain sight. Alexandria was the primary launching point for the new fusion religion we know as "Christianity" today. The word "Christos" is directly related to Krishna, Crestos, and Chreston. These literally mean "shining", as they refer to the sun. Krishna is the sun deity of the Hindu religion. Even as late as 348 CE, Cyrill said:
"Let the heresy be silenced which blasphemes the Messiah, the Son of the Mighty One. Let those be silenced who say that the sun is Messiah, because He is the Creator of the sun, and not the visible sun itself."
They were calling the sun "Christ Helios". The Manichaeans worshipped the sun as it passed through the sky ALL DAY, and Augustine came from them. The ancient Crestos of the Serapian Culte was worshipped as "the good god", so the word "Christ" is actually a polluted and forbidden

word when you carefully weigh the texts of Exodus 23:13 & Duet. 12:28-32. Great darkness results from not properly understanding YHWH's Word, or departing from it, thinking it no longer has application. The one verse most cling to in defense of the term "Christian" is at Acts 11:26:

"And at first in Antioch the taught ones were called Kristianous." (This is the **order** of this sentence in the Greek, literally quoted from the Greek interlinear).

This sentence doesn't claim that the disciples called *themselves* this, but were *called* this "at first". If this meant they were mistaken for the Pagan believers in Serapis, that's one thing; or this could have been simply the Greek *translation* distorting the original Hebrew word. But what if this Greek word was not a label, and simply meant "good men"? Knowing there is some relationship with the word **_cretin_**, what if the people of Antioch, at first, called the disciples **CRETINS**?

Why is the Greek label so important that they had to make this single verse in its translation an all-encompassing issue? Again, what would a bunch of Israelites that practice the Torah of YHWH and follow a Yahudi Messiah be doing with a Greek term used by Pagans as a label for themselves?

What great harm is there in abandoning the Greek title "Christos", and using the same Hebrew word Daniel wrote: Mashiach? The word "MESSIAH" is transliterated TWICE in the received Greek writings, at Jn. 1:41 and Jn. 4:25 (it's used twice in Daniel, at 9:25,26). Even the new age cult is awaiting their "Christ"; so why not give them their word back - maybe they'll stop laughing at believers behind their backs for having adopted so much of their philosophy. Give them their "Sunday" too. Let's return to the Covenant, shall we? The Gentiles from the ends of the Earth will one day acknowledge that their forefathers have inherited nothing but lies. *from teosofia.com/Mumbai/7502christmas.html we read further:*

*"**Krishna** or Chris-na and Christos come from the same root. **Kris** in Sanskrit means the pure or the sacred, 'the first emanation of the invisible G-dhead, manifesting itself tangibly in spirit' (Isis Unveiled, II, 158), it is the Spiritual Ego (Buddhi-Manas). .... 'The Spiritual, Immortal, Higher Ego in every man is an emanation, like a ray, from the Central Spiritual Sun (Paramatman), of which the visible Sun is the direct*

manifestation on our physical plane and its visible symbol.'"

The conclusion drawn from this study confirms once again that the faith was "solarized", and our customs and words are rising up to prove it. The prophet YermeYahu told us:

"O YHWH, my strength, and my fortress, and my refuge in the day of affliction, the Gentiles shall come unto thee from the ends of the Earth, and shall say, 'Surely our fathers have inherited lies, vanity, and things wherein there is no profit'.

Shall a man make elohim unto himself, and they are no elohim? Therefore, behold, I will this once cause them to know, I will cause them to know Mine hand and My might; and they shall know that My Name is YHWH." Jer 16:19-21

Directly related to this issue of "terms" once used by Pagans, and taking the point-of-view of our Creator Yahuah, we have to consider what He has already spoken on this issue. Remember, even the "terminology" used by Pagans are their "ways" or methods. Here are 3 Scriptures of many that could have relevance:

Exodus / Shemoth 20:2,3:
"I am Yahuah your Elohim, Who brought you out of the land of Mitsrayim, out of the house of slavery. You have no other mighty ones against My Face."

Exodus / Shemoth 23:13:
"And in all that I have said to you take heed. And make no mention of the name of other mighty ones, let it not be heard from your mouth."
So what about Woden'sDay, Thor'sDay, FriggaDay, etc.,?

Deut. / Debarim 12:28-32:
"Guard, and obey all these words which I command you, that it might be well with you and your children after you forever, when you do what is good and right in the eyes of Yahuah your Elohim. When Yahuah your Elohim does cut off from before you the nations which you go to dispossess, and you dispossess them and dwell in their land, guard yourself that you are not ensnared to follow them, after they are destroyed from before you, and that you do not inquire about their mighty ones, saying, 'How did these nations serve their mighty ones? And let me do

so too.' Do not do so to Yahuah your Elohim, for every abomination which Yahuah hates they have done to their mighty ones, for they even burn their sons and daughters in the fire to their mighty ones. All the words I am commanding you, guard to do it - do not add to it nor take away from it."

The conclusion drawn from this study confirms once again that the faith was "solarized", and our customs and words are rising up to prove it. The prophet YermeYahu told us:

"O YHWH, my strength, and my fortress, and my refuge in the day of affliction, the Gentiles shall come unto thee from the ends of the Earth, and shall say, 'Surely our fathers have inherited lies, vanity, and things wherein there is no profit'. Shall a man make elohim unto himself, and they are no elohim? Therefore, behold, I will this once cause them to know, I will cause them to know Mine hand and My might; and they shall know that My Name is YHWH."   Jer 16:19-21

"Yeshua" or "Yahushua"?

A Transliteration study on the Name of the Messiah (remember: Yahushua isn't a Christian, and His Name isn't based on Greek).

You will soon learn that the form "JESUS" is derived directly from "YESHU", explained below.   What "YESHU" means will change your thinking about this radically.

Q: Where did we get the form "JESUS" from?

A: The Jesuits   (They defend the form using the Greek and Latin, hoping you'll never discover what you are about to read):

The form "YESHUA" is from the acronym "YESHU", a mutilation of Yahushua's Name used by unbelieving Yahudim during the late 1st and 2nd century CE.   The letters in "YESHU" stood for the sentence, "may his name be blotted out" (from the scroll of life).   This "Yeshu" acronym is the real root of the form "JESUS", after going through Greek, then Latin:

YESHU (remember, this is an acronym, meaning "may his

TRANSLITERATION STUDY
The original Hebrew appearance of the Name of Mashiach
(with the closest letters in Greek below)

palaeo-Hebrew letters

Yahushua

ayin shin waw hay yod
shortened form: OYWꞱ Yahshua

Aramaic/modern Hebrew letters

Yahushua
yod

ayin shin waw hay
shortened form: ישוע Yahshua

Greek (still lacking correct sounds for yod and shin)

sound of
short form: IΑΣΟΥΑ

alpha   omikron   alpha
iota   sigma   upsilon

The omikron-upsilon combination allows for the "oo" sound,
making them form a "dipthong" in the Greek.

name be blotted out", referring to the scroll of life). A rabbinic word-play, from the original Hebrew words:

"Yemach Shmo u'Zikro"   NOTE: There's not actually a letter "W" in the Hebrew alef-beth; the letter "W" is a rather new letter to our own alpha-beta. It's called a "DOUBLE-U" for a reason; our letter "U" is a perfect match with the sixth letter of the Hebrew alef-beth, now called a "WAW".

Acronyms are abbreviated messages, like "SCUBA" stands for "self contained underwater breathing apparatus".

YESU IESOU - Going into Greek, the letter "Y" became an IOTA because Greek has no "Y"; also, the sound of "SH" was lost, because Greek has no letters to make this sound. The letter combination "OU" is a diphthong, arising from the Greek attempt to transliterate the sound "OO" as in "woof". Our letter "U" and the Hebrew letter "WAW" does this easily.

YESOUS IESOU took on an ending "S" to form IESOUS, since the Greek wanted to render the word masculine with the ending "S". Going to Latin, the diphthong "OU" became "U".

JESUS In the early 1530's, the letter "J" developed, causing a tail on proper names beginning with the letter " i ", and words used at the beginning of sentences.   This "J" is really the letter "IOTA".   Many European languages pronounce "J" as the letter " i ", or a "Y" sound.   They even spell Yugoslavia this way: *"Jugoslavia"*.

Now you know.   Tell everyone you know, and don't allow the Jesuits to succeed at this horrifying deception.   Yeh-Zeus is not our Messiah;
(The true name, Yahushua, means Yah-is our-salvation)

NIXON & ELVIS MERGED!

IF YOU BELIEVE THE KIND OF NONSENSE THIS REPRESENTS, YOU MIGHT BE LED TO BELIEVE THE MESSIAH OF ISRAEL HAS A GREEK NAME.

YOU CAN GET YOUR COUNTRY AND YOUR GOSPEL ALL FROM THE SAME GUY NOW!

No one would believe this nonsense, yet this same kind of thinking produces the belief that the Messiah has a <u>Greek</u> name. And a Greek title.   They even want to label <u>themselves</u> with the Greek title.   We've all fallen victim to the Theater of the Absurd; now it's time to correct all that.

To see the reactions of seminary-trained men on this topic, read the article beginning on page 78, *Response to Critics*.

The question was posed, "Can we transliterate Messiah's Name (Yahshua) back into the Greek?"

It's a reasonable challenge, and it could be fun to do; but it may not prove anything one way or the other. Going through the motions will help us appreciate the difficulty getting alphabets to interface with one another, and perhaps help emphasize the importance of putting our trust in the original autographs, not the transitional language of Greek. Mashiach Yahushua was not given a Greek name, but a well-recognized Hebrew Name, yod-hay-waw-shin-ayin, and spelled yod-shin-waw-ayin in it's shortened form. One has to understand the distinction between transliteration and translation.

I think it's a good idea for us all to take a little time looking at the results of the "reverse transliteration" process, to help us get closer to some names and words; however the "flaw" is thinking we can reach through foreign alphabets which have intermediate distortions of letters, and grammar rules which have no application to the original language. But, for the fun of it, it's not a bad idea at all. I wanted to take the word "DUDE" and transliterate it into Hebrew. Oddly enough, taking this word to the Hebrew alphabet simply involves 3 letters: dalet-waw-dalet -- which spells the name of the famous king of Israel known as "DAVID". In Hebrew, we have been led to believe this word is the name "DAVID", or even "DAWID". Actually, either of these transliterations could be slightly off, or different from the original word meaning "beloved" in Hebrew. It may be that the sound of the Hebrew letters, dalet-waw-dalet, is in fact, "DUDE", or "DA'UD". It is very closely associated, it seems, with the Hebrew word for "breast", "DAD" (with a short sounding letter "A"). There are plenty of Arabian folks running around (probably Ishmaelites, even some Edomites*) who are called by Hebrew names; one you may see often is "YUSEF", or YOSEF. Another name that is popular with these Arabs is DA'UD. So, perhaps my theory that the Hebrew letter we call "waw" is far from being anything like our modern letter "W", and is more like our familiar letter "U". "W" is called "*double-U*"; so maybe we need to think of the "waw" as a single "U", since it seems to sound like one in

* *EDOMITES* - DECENDANTS OF **ESAU**; *EDOMIM*

so many Hebrew words. The phrase "HALLELU YAH" uses this same Hebrew letter called "waw" to give the "U" sound. The name of the tribe "YAHUDAH" gives us the same result (yod-hay-waw-dalet-hay) -- and this is the same spelling, and order, for the Creator's personal Name, with the addition of the letter dalet.

If we go to the Greek language, and attempt to spell YAHSHUA, the first thing we notice is that we cannot do it for the lack of two letter/sounds: the **Y** and the **SH**. But, if we had to come as close as we possibly could, it would still wind up like trying to play a symphony on a 4-string banjo. It would have to begin with the Greek letter IOTA, then to simulate the vowel sound in "YAH" the second Greek letter would have to be an ALPHA. Clement of Alexandria spelled YA-HUAH (yod-hay-waw-hay) with the Greek letters *IAOUE*.

So, we have the first letters in the Greek being *IA*. The next step is to make the only choice left to us for the "SH" sound: SIGMA. Finally, I would choose the final letters as UPSILON and ALPHA. You can see these Greek letters and their sounds at the following website: http://www.ibiblio.org/koine/greek/lessons/alphabet.html

Perhaps the upsilon alone would not be enough, but to make the sound of the Hebrew waw (oo as in "food"), we would need to link it with the omikron to make a "dipthong", OU, then add the ending sound A (alpha). It would be best to simply ignore the Greek rule to make the word masculine (this would add an ending "S").

Now we have the Greek letters IOTA, ALPHA, SIGMA, OMIKRON, UPSILON, ALPHA. The only aberrations this leaves is the first letter IOTA, and the SIGMA. This only makes the best attempt to sound the SHORT form of Mashiach's full-blown Name (YAHUSHUA), shortening it to YAHSHUA (or the popularized Y'shua). The best the Greek can do is make it sound something like "IASUA" (if we transliterate the Greek into Latin letters, like the ones we use in English, which is frighteningly close to IESU, based on YESHU described above.

Writing is perhaps the most important human invention; but it's objective is to record/document the sounds of letters.

Where we lose information and accuracy is where alphabets interface with one another. The Greek language is nothing short of a meat grinder to certain letter sounds. So, we each should study enough to answer the question, "Can we transliterate Messiah's Name (Yahshua) back into the Greek?" The more I've looked into it, the answer is no; it's just a matter of how much mutilation a person is willing to accept -- toward the Name above all names.

When people readily argue over their beloved word, JESUS, let them know that the Geneva "Bible" didn't use the spelling JESUS because the letter "J" didn't even exist at the time. The spelling was IESUS, a Latinization *based on Greek*. The Authorized Version (KJV) is the first English translation to use this word, JESUS. Prior to the 16th century, the best "sound" of the Name for our Mashiach was "YESU" for over 1000 years. But now, the Truth is being shouted from the rooftops, and what was kept secret is being revealed to all who study and search out everything they believe. There really is "buried treasure" to be discovered through personal study.

Scholars, etymology experts, and theologians will not disagree with you about other Hebrew names' true transliterations. "James" is really *"Ya'aqob"*, "John" is really *"Yahuchanon"*, and "Isaiah" is really *"Yesha Yahu"*. But, when you want to use the correct Name for the Mashiach of Israel, they may get red-faced and defensive of their "Jesus" derived from YESHU. Could there be a spiritual stronghold involved in the use of the word "Jesus"? If you know it to be a lie, then stop calling your Mashiach this false name. Call Him by His real Name, the Name above all names: YAHUSHUA. It's the same spelling in Hebrew (YOD-HAY-WAW-SHIN-AYIN) used for the successor of Mosheh whom they call "Joshua", as anyone can see even the Greek letters match for both at Acts 7 and Hebrews 4.

Yeast (or leaven) of the Pharisees (or Prushim)
Yeast is something that puffs-up, or adds - changing the volume of what it is corrupting.

Did you know that the *Samaritans* (those of the apostate, rebellious 10 tribes in the north of the land of Israel, in

Samaria) had ELEVEN COMMANDMENTS in their system of observance? (We'll talk more about that in the next article). The first Ten Commandments were the same, but the 11th was a man-made command that they were to assemble only at **Mt. Gerizim**, NOT YERUSHALIYIM. They "puffed it up". Well, it's interesting that Catholicism made some changes too. Other Christian denominations restored some things, but the denominations have been making excuses about which Commandments apply to them.

We are going to see individuals within many Christian congregations learn they are the lost sheep of the **House of Israel** in the coming years, as they move toward the **Torah**, learn the **Name**, and realize who they are in Yahushua. They will receive a *love for the Torah* (the Truth, YHWH's Word), which is inviting Yahushua to **write the 10 Commandments on their heart**, which **is** the New Covenant (or re-newed Covenant). They will engraft into **Israel**, by being immersed into the New Covenant (or re-newed Covenant), and know they are branches (Natsarim) in the olive tree *(the natural olive tree, **ISRAEL** - Romans 11 - we don't remain "wild" olive branches, but are engrafted into the natural one).* Scripture calls the lost tribes of Israel by several terms. They are called "Israel", and sometimes "Ephraim" as we see at Jeremiah 31. They were also called "**Samaritans**", since they lived in the region called *Samaria*. The *House of Israel* (the 10 tribes in the north, in Samaria) was carried away by the Assyrians over 120 years BEFORE the *House of Yahudah* was taken away by the Babylonians in 586 BCE. The "House of Israel" is distinguished from the "House of Yahudah" when you study Jeremiah chapter 3, and here these 2 "houses" are called "sisters". This is why we have two "olive trees" discussed in various places. They will be restored to ONE STICK (or more accurately, TREE, from the word etz), Ezekiel 37. For now, Ephraim, or the House of Israel, is dispersed among the NATIONS (Amos 9:9). They can legitimately be called Samaritans, and this is why Yahushua gave the parable about the "**Good Samaritan**". The parable about the **prodigal son** was also about these lost sheep dispersed among the nations (Amos 9:9). While the "houses" are called "sisters" in Jeremiah 3, the parable of the **prodigal son** describes them as two brothers. They are the **"other sheep who are not of** *this fold*" (as distinguished from the Yahudim), but still very much of Israel! As it was when the 12 tribes of Israel left Egypt, today there are those of a "mixed multitude" among believers, but all who engraft into Israel become as native-born Israelites. We are of every race, so we cannot tell by outward physical appearance who is an Israelite; those born of Father YHWH obey His Torah, and by this we know who is our brother and sister.

Ephraimites, the lost tribes of the House of Israel, or the Samaritans, are coming back to Father YHWH's Covenant 10 Words (Torah), and the Hebraic Roots movement is growing rapidly -- Christians are becoming "Messianic" more and more. As you know, there is simultaneously a growing interest in the Talmud (oral law, Mishnah/Gemara) among Messianic Natsarim. The Talmud costs several thousand dollars for a complete set of its volumes. Many defend it's validity for study, since it does provide a great deal of insight into what certain things meant to those living long ago. I, for one, understand that it was over the "oral laws" that Rabbi Yahushua had many disputes with the Pharisees, although they were close in so many other ways. These "customs of the elders" which added to the Torah conflicted with the Torah, replaced it, and added burdens to the "light yoke". When the Temple was completely destroyed by the army of Titus in 70 CE, the control (power, authority) over how to function religiously shifted from the Sadducees to the Pharisees, because they held the hearts of the common people in the out-lying synagogues. The Pharisees held closely to Torah, but they revered the "traditions" of the fathers to be almost as important. This is the "oral law", commonly known as the TALMUD.

The Talmud is not a book; it's a record of questions, debates, and decisions over a *1200-year period*. One could think of it as if there were a board of directors making decisions over a 1200 year-long corporate meeting, and the Talmud is the "minutes" of that meeting. There is a Babylonian Talmud, and a Jerusalem Talmud. The former is usually the one that is quoted, and is magnitudes larger. It is entirely of human invention, and definitely not to be confused with inspired Scripture, the Words of YHWH. In it you will find how to best (in man's view) tie tzitzith, rest on Shabbath, and pray. But, the Talmud will tell you to *never pronounce* the Name of

Yahuah aloud -- and proclaims the death penalty for doing so. It claims Yahushua's mother was a whore, and He is the offspring of a Roman soldier. It says both Yahushua and His mother Miryam are being punished in a very unsavory place. Talmud says that a man who has sexual intercourse with a young girl who is not mature is the same as the girl hurting herself on a stick -- and that it is as nothing at all. With men writing such things as this, how can we possibly put our trust in their judgments? We cannot trust in man (Ps. 118:8).

This body of work is filled with things we *could* gain insights from, but at the same time it is a very poor guide to consult for definitive answers as to how we should live -- the Torah is our sole resource for how to live a pleasing life for YHWH, not Talmud. The Talmud is not what we live by, and it is packed with all kinds of issues we could argue over. I'm sure if we pleased Talmud promoters in one area, there would be hundreds of new issues from it to argue over, enough to last us thousands of years.

So, we need to also be careful to note the "yeast" and puffing-up which we may observe in others as they grow in knowledge. The Talmud seems to be the best candidate among us for being this "yeast of the Pharisees", since from these early Pharisees (Prushim) all of Rabbinical Judaism sprang forth. The Torah is a light "yoke", but the Talmud certainly isn't light. Our "older brothers" in Rabbinical Yahudaism have traditionally been steeped in the Talmud, but our love of the "older brother", those of Yahudah, must be ever present with us, because anyone who does not love his brother does not have the love of YHWH. That doesn't mean we have to love the yeast / teachings of the Talmud also. The reason this is so much of an issue to me is because I visited 3 brothers whom I assisted in immersion over 15 years ago; they were studying the Talmud when I walked in, and the Torah was nowhere to be seen. I couldn't persuade them to see what was happening. If this goes on with others, then the Talmud will be spreading among us so fast it will cause division among us.

I feel Rabbi Yahushua gave us the warning to beware of this yeast. His students thought He was talking about bread, and at first didn't understand what He meant. We all need to stay vigilant and not be deceived or misled by teachings from the Talmud. The prohibition of uttering the Name comes from the Talmud. It adds to the words of Torah. It's human error disguised as Truth. Oddly, most try to justify using the spelling "Yahweh" by citing the Jewish Encyclopedia, yet it is obvious this is just a shade away from the actual sound because the TALMUD prohibits the utterance of the Name, and the Jewish scholars revere Talmud. (I don't mean to be critical of those who believe "Yahweh" is the most correct sound! It's just that there should be 3 syllables, and the "litmus test" is another Hebrew word, YAHUDAH -- the same letters in the same order, with an added "dalet". The word YAHUDAH is the doorway to the actual sound). The 3 syllables reflect the meaning of the Name; *"I was, I am, and I will be"*. Revelation 1:8 identifies the meaning as *"Who is and Who was and Who is to come, the Almighty"*. He is "omnitemporal", since He exists in all of time, or "at all times". This unique Hebrew word, yod-hay-waw-hay, contains all 3 "tenses".

An example of the **Talmud**:
"Now, there was in the Temple a stone on which was engraved the Tetragrammaton [YHWH] or Schem Hamphorasch, that is to say, the Ineffable Name of God; this stone had been found by King David when the foundations of the Temple were being prepared and was deposited by him in the Holy of Holies. **Jeschu** (YESHU), *knowing this, came from Galilee and, penetrating into the Holy of Holies, read the Ineffable name, which he transcribed on to a piece of whom parchment and concealed in an incision under his skin. By this means he was able to work miracles and to persuade the people that he was the son of God foretold by Isaiah. With the aid of Judas, the Sages of the Synagogue, succeeding in capturing Jeschu, who was then lead before the Great and Little Sanhedrim, by whom he was condemned to be stoned to death and finally hanged."* Such is the story of Christ according to the Jewish Kabbalists ..." (treatise Sabbath, folio 104, treatise Sanhedrim, folio 107, and Sota, folio 47).

Anything that adds to the Torah is leaven, and is potentially dangerous. The "oral law" became the "Babylonian Talmud" and the "Jerusalem Talmud", made up of the Mishnah, and the Gemara. These Pharisaical sources were the seeds of Rabbinical Judaism.

When Yahushua told us, **"Beware of the LEAVEN of the Pharisees"** (Luke 12:1, Mk. 8:15, Mt. 16:6), He was describing the hidden mysticisms of the Zohar, Kabbala, and the Sefer Yetzirah (oral laws). The Talmud states that Yahushua was the bastard son of a Roman soldier, and that He and His mother (Miryam) are boiling in excrement at this very moment, as eternal punishment for their sins. Yet we sometimes see Messianic teachers QUOTE from other texts in the Talmud. It's not a pure spring to drink from -- so stay away from it. "Wormwood" is poisoned Living Water. The Truth is mixed with error, and can still kill you. The Torah specifically prohibits ADDING to YHWH's Words, which the Talmud in fact does. All of His Words were "*READ ALOUD*" in the hearing of the people, so that rules out any other words orally transmitted. Those in certain "Messianic" circles have traditionally shunned pronouncing the Name aloud, to keep from "offending" their fellows who adhered to the Talmudic prohibition against the Name, and who used the traditional titles instead. Essentially, they are "no-namers". They forsake the feelings of our Father YHWH, in deference to pleasing their fellow man. This is the root of why there is some division between us -- we are not ONE because we have not kept away from the leaven of the Pharisees, the Talmud -- some of us have shunned the Name, which is to keep us in unity. We are divided over the Name, and those who use it are sometimes dubbed "cultists" and heretics. Rabbinical Judaism stemmed directly from the Pharisees, and is just as filled with the errors of the Oral Law as ever. The customs of the "fathers" (manmade human traditions from the oral law) were the hypocrisy which Yahushua kept throwing up to the Pharisees and Sadducees. Torah has outlawed it, but it persists. I will be attacked for having said this about the "oral law", but I must take a stand for Truth -- and let every man be proven a liar, and YHWH's Word True.

The Talmud (Oral Law) has no bearing on Natsarim. Quoting from it should be done with words of warning. We can read anything, but we must be discerning. Yahushua's words as recorded in the Brit Chadasha only make sense to those His Spirit indwells, and He will guide us into all that is True. When He told His pupils "beware of the leaven of the

Pharisees", it was the "leaven" (puffing-up, adding) that was their main stumbling block -- and it's the oral traditions. Sure, there are many historical explanations found buried in Talmudic sources, but there are also dark mixtures of Kabbalistic influences as well. It speaks of when to stone "blasphemers". Pronouncing the Name is blasphemy to this work of hypocrisy, this idol to men's wisdom. Yahudim "mysticism" and other Babylonian / Chaldean syncretisms are blending into the Talmud, coming from the Zohar (Splendor), Bahir (Brilliance), and Sefer Yetzirah (Book of Creation). These influences gave rise to the customs like washing the fingertips before eating (to wash away evil spirits). The bottom line is, the Torah forbids studying other sources and mixing them into the worship of Him (see Duet. 12:28-32), which is also why we cannot observe Christmas, Easter, and other things like "Sun-Day".

In my opinion, we can read anything with the discernment of Yahushua's Spirit in us to guard against doctrinal errors. The comment He made concerning drinking "**deadly poison**" can be understood to refer to **false teaching**, which is poison. The teachings of men are literally filled with teachings of death and darkness, yet men profess they contain wisdom. **Kabbala** and **Talmud** are woven with many things of darkness, and draw away many with their dark "secrets". Yahushua insulted the teachers of 2000 years ago when He told them that **a child** could easily understand more than they could, because there are no dark secrets being concealed. Those who look deeply into the understandings of men are being led astray, and they are wasting their time.

My advice is to not waste a moment of your time studying Kabbalah, but warn others of it's dangers. The Talmud conveys information that stems from Kabbala in part.
The following are a few texts which co-relate the tongue (teachings) with deadly poison:

Mark 16:17-18:
"And these signs will accompany those who believe: In My Name they will drive out demons; they will speak in new tongues; they will pick up snakes with their hands; and when they drink deadly poison, it will not hurt them at all; they will place their hands on sick people, and they will get well."

Romans 3:13-14:

"Their throats are open graves; their tongues practice deceit."

"The poison of vipers is on their lips. Their mouths are full of cursing and bitterness."

James 3:7-8:   (James is really Ya'aqob)

"All kinds of animals, birds, reptiles and creatures of the sea are being tamed and have been tamed by man, but no man can tame the tongue. It is a restless evil, full of deadly poison."

Torah (YHWH's Word, Teaching) instructs us not to "ADD" or take away from Torah, and the "leaven" of Talmud is exactly this, whether or not a pastor, rabbi, teacher, or leader sees it this way. All the Words of YHWH were READ aloud in the hearing of the people -- there were no words that were "oral" -- this is only the TRADITIONAL mindset of flawed and misguided men. Torah knows nothing of the Talmud, and it makes no references to the other books I cited above. The Talmud is OK to own and read; but we have no time to use it as study material when Yahushua told us to beware of it. The only thing it is good for is understanding what went wrong with Yahudaism; and mainly, it was the Talmud! This is the source of where folks get many ideas foreign to Scripture. The religion of Yahudaism (Judaism) followed along the lines of Pharisaical teachings, and the Talmud became the record book of their decisions over the centuries. There is the Yerushaliyim Talmud, and the Babylonian Talmud. If any group leader is insisting on spending any time on it as 'serious study' and not exposing the problems with it in spite of the dangers, this letter should be taken to the group (body), to make sure it is well understood what is happening among everyone. You can't mix clean water and poison together and drink it. That's wormwood. Hey, even Pagan religions had some truth in them!

The Talmud   ~ there is the **Babylonian Talmud** (Talmud Babli), which is the most commonly referred to; and there is the **Talmud J**, or **Jerusalem Talmud**, which is much shorter and incomplete, and has not been preserved entirely. The **Talmud Babli** contains over 2,500,000 words, over 3 times the **Talmud J**. The Talmud Babli is usually at least 35 volumes, and is not a "book", but an immense record of questions, answers, and arguments, similar, as I said, to a record of the minutes of a court or board of directors, taken over a period of 1200 years (from the 5th century before, to the 8th century after, the Christian common era). It is a _monumental seminar_ of decisions, based on the _opinions_ of over 2000 scholar/rabbis, and it applies itself partly to the study of Torah, with commentaries and debates. Another way of looking at it is, it comprises much of what was referred to as the "oral law", or "traditions of the elders/fathers", but in written form.

True, it explores wisdom, truth, ethics, laws, hygiene, medicine, history, metaphysics, pedagogy, and virtue; but it is often quaint, parochial, and superstitious. Within it we can learn things, certainly. But, it is not to be compared with inspired Scripture. It describes Yahushua as the bastard son of a Roman soldier, and states that both He and His mother (Miryam) at this moment are boiling in excrement as punishment for their foul lives. It forbids the utterance of the Name of our Creator, yod-hay-waw-hay (a violation of the 3rd Commandment). This is much more serious than telling Scotty that the Enterprise is a garbage scow (In one episode of Star Trek, a Klingon told Scotty this, and it started a fight - and yes, I know about the New Age underpinnings of the Star Wars and Star Trek). The "_laws of men_" (human opinions) which set aside the **Words of YHWH** in order to satisfy human traditions is one charge that could certainly be made, and this charge _was_ made by our Messiah, Yahushua. The fact that the Talmud **adds** to the yoke of Torah, and **adds** to the inspired Word of YHWH, is the weightier matter. The distinction is that Torah is the teaching of YHWH through His prophets and emmissaries, and Talmud is made up of the teachings and **opinions** passed down from men. The only yoke we as Natsarim are obliged to carry is the light yoke of Torah, without the Talmud.

The Talmud is divided into 4 catagories; (1) Mishnah (interpretations of Scripture passed down orally, court decisions, and rituals) -- (2) the Midrash and Haggada (lessons in homely, amusing, and poetic ways), -- (3) the Gemara (meaning "completion") which is a commentary on the Mishnah, and (4) the Responsa (based on letters sent to scholars asking for interpretations and rulings on Torah -- contemporary data as it related to philosophical disputes, intellectual life, historical events, or social conditions.   So, my love for the **Torah** does not extend to the Talmud.

ROMANS   The entire book of Romans is Shaul's writing to a synagogue in Rome, containing both Israelites _born_ into the faith furthering their studies, and _converting_ Gentiles. Of this group, many came to believe in Yahushua as Mashiach, and Shaul begins by pointing out the **evidence** of the "Messiah-ship" of Yahushua: His **resurrection from the dead**. He reviews the obvious existence of a Creator, since all of creation provides the evidence of an Intelligent Designer.   Shaul paints broad strokes, and in chapter 2 discusses the reprobate minds of those who reject the Truth and evidence all around them, causing men to burn with desire for each other, leaving the natural heterosexual relationship with women as one example of their depravity. He says even their _women_ will abandon their natural function.

By the time we get to chapters 6, 7, & 8, Shaul describes the **Brith Chadasha**, or "re-newed" Covenant, contrasting walking in the flesh, and walking in the Spirit. Our conversion involves a shift in what we desire, and he carefully explains the operation of how the "re-newed" Covenant works over these 3 chapters.

By chapter 11, Shaul dives into the fact that there is a calling to both the native-born to the Covenant (Yisrael, the natural, good olive tree), as well as foreigners (wild olive tree), and calls these two groups "branches".   Some of the natural branches don't accept Mashiach, and so are not connected to the Root, which is Mashiach, the source of the Life, and are "broken-off" branches. The natural olive tree is Yisrael, and is made up of both the Root (Mashiach) and the branches, all 12 tribes. This "whole" is one complete olive tree, so since 2 become "one flesh", Yisrael can also be the Mashiach -- however this label should _include_ His bride/wife, the tribes. Along with these tribes, a **mixed multitude** from among the nations "engraft" into Yisrael, because they convert to the path/walk we call **Torah**, which Yahushua is -- the "living Word/debar", which is "living water".   It is living and active, and is Yahushua's living Spirit in the believers who obey (Acts 5:32). Once "engrafted" into the natural / good olive tree, there is _no distinction_ between a native-born Yisraelite and a former

"foreigner" -- all are set-apart, selected, _chosen_, and connected to the source, the Root which gives life to the
branches. The fruit of this is love, joy, peace, patience, kindness, goodness, gentleness, faithfulness, and self-control.
For Gentiles, there is _no hope_ without joining Yisrael. When
you obey the Covenant (Ten Words), then you are Yisrael. If
you stop obeying them, you're _cut off_ from Yisrael. You don't
need any man's "permission" to obey the Covenant; it's only
between you and Yahushua. If you obey the Covenant, you
have fellowship with YHWH, **_and_** with one another. Without
the Covenant, there is no fellowship -- and the Commandments are the _keys_ to the Kingdom. Ignoring them is why
there are so many diverse "denominations" in the world.
There is only one, correct "denomination", and it is Yisrael --
the 12 gates into the New Yerushalayim are each named for a
tribe of Yisrael, and not a single gate for Christians is mentioned. The threshold foundation stones are named for each
of the 12 emissaries (apostles). Those who enter these
gates are Yisraelites, whether they came from Gentile stock
or not --

*"Blessed are those _doing_ His Commands, so that the
authority shall be theirs unto the tree of life and to enter
through the gates into the city."* REVELATION 22:14

So, while we divide ourselves into boxes/denominations
now, it won't matter which box we kept ourselves trapped in
during our fleshly lives when everyone is in the world-to-
come. This means simply that there is certainly no excuse to
be in any "denomination" (other than Yisrael) _now_. Either you
are Yisrael, or you are not. Not being joined and counted as
Yisrael leaves only one possibility, and that's the crowd
"outside", called "dogs", who are not allowed to enter the
gates.

Yahushua ha-Mashiach has a "way" or "path" called Torah
which He writes on the hearts of those who accept Him. Others may have a "religion" which is certainly "about" Him, but it
may easily not be HIS way -- someone made it up, mixing
Paganism (idolatry) with Him, causing masses to be in a stupor, having drunk of the "wine" of the harlot. When Truth is
mixed with error/doctrines of demons (Paganism/Satanism),
it's like clean water mixed with poison. This is ultimately

deadly, and Scripture calls it "wormwood". Listening to dark-ness and light mixed together will keep the listener in a drunken stupor. The solution is to stay away from the "denominational" boxes, and do personal study in the Scrip-tures. Study will quickly cause the person to "see", and have great differences in their understanding so much so that lis-tening to the lies they were used to hearing will actually be painful to bear.

The "firstfruits" spoken of at Romans 11:16 is Mashiach, and Shaul describes Him as the Root, which makes the branches connected to Him also set-apart. The Hebrew word "qodesh" means set-apart or selected/chosen, and not pro-fane or common. So, a "qodeshi" would be one who is a _living_, selected individual, commonly called a "saint". The plu-ral, "qodeshim", could be understood as "saints". These are chosen, and both believe **and** obey the Commandments of YHWH, as we see Rev. 14:

"Here is the endurance of the set-apart ones (Qodeshim, saints), here are those who are guarding the Command-ments of Elohim _and_ the belief of Yahushua."
REVELATION 14:12 (see also Rev. 12:17).

"Blessed are those doing His Commands, so that the au-thority shall be theirs unto the tree of life and to enter through the gates into the city." REVELATION 22:14

The Samaritans . . . and the 11th Commandment

The land of northern Israel was also known as **Samaria**. This "Samaria" is where 10 of the 12 tribes of Israel once called home - and they were called "**Samaritans**", as people are often known by _where_ they are from. Each tribe had been given a portion of the land as an inheritance (except for the tribe Lewi, who lived among the other tribes all over the land). The "Samaritans" were indeed Israel - 10 tribes of it in fact! Scripture refers to these 10 tribes in the northern area, Samaria, as the "**House of Israel**". We know that they were scattered, but will one day be regathered (Ezek. 37).

Abshalom, the son of Da'ud, caused the beginning of a division between the northern 10 tribes, and the 2 tribes in the south around Yerushalyim. Eventually, the "Samaritans" rebelled against the authority of the southern king at Yerusha-

Iyim, and then hatred developed between the north and the south. The north became known as the "House of Israel", and was sometimes referred to as "Ephraim". The south became known as the "*House of Yahudah*". The main contention between them was over WHERE to gather to observe the festivals of Unleavened Bread, Shabuoth, and Tabernacles (Sukkoth). So, to control the population, the Samaritan rulers created an 11th Commandment, or the 614th Torah ordinance. The 11th commandment in the Samaritan Pentateuch: *"Thou shalt worship YHWH your Elohim in Mount Gerizim"*

Recall that Yahushua's conversation with the Samaritan woman at the well involved this *"11th Commandment"* Yn. 4:19-24: *"The woman said to Him, 'Master, I see that You are a prophet. Our fathers worshipped on this mountain, but you (people) say that in Yerushalyim is the place where one needs to worship.' Yahushua said to her, 'Woman, believe Me, the hour is coming when you shall neither on this mountain, nor in Yerushalyim, worship the Father. You worship what you do not know. We worship what we know, because the deliverance is of the Yahudim. But the hour is coming, and now is, when the true worshippers shall worship the Father in spirit and truth, for the Father also does seek such to worship Him. Elohim is Spirit, and those who worship Him need to worship in spirit and truth.'"* (Those of you who are being pressured to go to a SPECIFIC place 3 times a year should read that 11th Commandment above, and weigh it in your heart whether or not you are listening to Yahushua, or your flawed leader's voice). Where TWO or more are gathered, Yahushua said, "I will be there".

The "Samaritans" or "House of Israel" was apostate, in rebellion; but be mindful, the Samaritans were not "foreigners", but were (and are) Israelites. They built a second Temple, or shrine, on Mount Gerizim. And, they added an eleventh Commandment to the Covenant - a major mistake. They also forbade the people of Samaria from observing the festivals at Yerushalyim, and appointed their own kohenim (priests), all of which contributed to their being ensnared by the Assyrian invaders. The northern tribes were attacked and scattered by the Assyrians in 722 BCE, but

YHWH knows where they are even after 2700+ years.

Ephraim is an important tribe to study, if you want to have your finger on the pulse of end-time events. They're not "Jews", simply because they are not of the _tribe_ of Yahudah. Remember Yosef? He had 2 sons while he was ruler in Mitsrayim (Egypt): Manasseh (1st born) and Ephraim (2nd born). The mother of both boys was the Egyptian girl who was given to Yosef to be his wife. Among the 12 tribes of Ya'aqob (Israel), Reuben _was_ the **"first born",** but his status was taken from him because he defiled his father's bed by sleeping with one of the wives of his father. Later, when Yosef brought Manasseh and **Ephraim** before Israel to receive his blessing, **Ephraim** received the blessing of the firstborn when Israel crossed his arms over the 2 boys' heads (see also Yirme Yahu 31:9, as this is all directly related to the Renewed Covenant). The older brother, the firstborn son, is the one who _expects_ the blessing as the firstborn; but when there is uncleanness or anything corrupt in that firstborn son, we see that the _younger brother_ will be selected to receive this cherished blessing. Sometimes it is simply the will of the father to give the younger son the blessing of the firstborn.

In the parable of the Prodigal Son, we see there are 2 brothers also, corresponding to the two houses of Israel. The older son stays home in the Father's household (keeps Torah). The _younger son_ takes what he is due as an inheritance, and _leaves the household_ (no longer observes Torah). Amos 9:9 tells us this: **_"For look, I am commanding, and I shall sift the house of Israel among all the Gentiles, as one sifts with a sieve, yet not a grain falls to the ground."_** This "house of Israel" refers to the **Samaritans**, the lost 10 tribes, also generally called "Ephraim". So, where's Ephraim? They are **sown into the Gentiles**, and they are returning as the Prodigal Son now (Acts 15, Eph. 3). The attention the Prodigal Son receives from the Father troubles the "older brother". But now we can understand _why_ a little better; Ephraim also has the status of "firstborn", even though he has been living for generations as an apostate "Gentile" -- raised by Gentiles! In the same chapter which prophesies the "Renewed Covenant" with the house of Israel _and_ the house of Yahudah (the same 2 sons as in the parable), YermeYahu 31, we read at verse 6: **_"For there shall be a day when the_** *watchmen cry on Mount Ephraim, 'Arise, and let us go up to Tsiyon, to YHWH our Elohim'."* Jer. 31:6.   The "watchmen" are "NATSARIM" -- the *same word* used in this Hebrew text which *we refer to ourselves today with*.   We guard the Commandments of YHWH, *and* hold to the testimony of Yahushua.   The term "Mount Ephraim" is everywhere the foundation of Ephraim is, which they cry out from and return (repent) to the Father's household, His **Torah**. Ephraim is literally *everywhere*, and they are now repenting and leaving the pig pens (false worship).   The parable of the Prodigal Son describes a **"famine"** where Ephraim has been living; this is living without the Commandments, the Bread of Life, the Living **Torah**.   His Father's house has this Bread, the Covenant Ten Commandments, which are *written upon our hearts by the Messiah*, Who now lives in us who repent, believe, and **obey** His Torah (Acts 5:32).

Yes, the people of Ephraim are currently living among people of unclean lips, but they are hungry for the Word (Torah, Commandments) of their Father's household, and this same Bread gives life to all those who eat of it.   This "bread" is not about "belief" only; one must also "<u>do</u>" the Word, or they are faking, lying, and/or simply deceived.   They cannot obey without receiving Yahushua, Who enables them to walk in the Spirit.   They know they cannot obey while walking in the flesh, nor do they have any desire to obey!

Of all the tribes of Israel, *Ephraim* holds the status and entitlements of the firstborn - directly bestowed upon him and his descendants by Israel, the father of the 12 tribes. While the Samaritans have been thoroughly dispersed among the Gentiles long ago as part of YHWH's plan (or secret), the "older brother" the Yahudim (or house of Yahudah) were also dispersed into the seed of the Gentiles.   When the house of Yahudah was carried away by the Babylonians in 586 BCE, only 10% returned to rebuild Yerushalyim after their 70 years of captivity.   So, all 12 tribes are lost; and the "older brother" cannot discern who this returning fellow is at all.   But, let's be loving, patient, kind, and gentle with people as they try to comprehend who we are.   They may initially attempt to fit us into a "box", or label us with a term they already understand. But, we have escaped from the box, or any pig pen (denominational prison) formerly designed to hold us;   we have been set free, because we have accepted a most precious gift: a love of the Truth. The King of the universe in coming, to establish His reign on the Earth. It will replace the man-made rulers and governments with the Torah. Yahushua's Name will be **Yahuah Tsedekenu**, not "Jesus". When parents and grandparents tell you, *"I had my religion all figured out long before you were born",* kindly remind them that Nimrod the tyrant had his religion all figured out long before **they** were born, and much of it has been passed down in the traditions they've embraced. YHWH is providing for the world to repent now, because His reign is drawing near. The shepherds are speaking, so listen to them, everyone:

"And I shall give you shepherds according to My heart, and they shall feed you with knowledge and understanding. And it shall be, when you have increased, and shall bear fruit in the land in those days, declares YHWH, that they no longer say, 'The ark of the Covenant of YHWH' Neither would it come to heart, nor would they remember it, nor would they visit it, nor would it be made again. At that time Yerushalyim shall be called the throne of YHWH, and all the nations shall be gathered to it, to the Name of YHWH, to Yerushalyim, and no longer walk after the stubbornness of their evil heart.
In those days the House of Yahudah shall go to the House of Yisrael, and they shall come together out of the land of the north to the land that I have given as an inheritance to your fathers." YermeYahu 3:15-18

If we interpret Yahushua's parable correctly, the two sons represent the two houses, beit Yahudah and beit Yisrael. The two houses are to be at odds with one another, be reconciled, and made into "one stick" according to several prophetic texts, most especially Ez. 37 (note v. 22). The Mashiach, Yahushua, is restoring them now, since we can see the returning son (lost tribes, Samaritans) awakening to Torah. The Father is drawing them. The older son that has rejected a belief in Yahushua has only rejected the anti-Torah "Christ" of Christianity. But the true Mashiach, the "Master of ha'Shabbat", is being brought to the older brother by the returning son. The prophecy of the "two sticks" becoming one in YHWH's hand would surely involve the Mashiach, since beit Yahudah must "engraft" once again as the natural branches that were broken off due to unbelief. So, in the parable of the Prodigal Son, when the son returns to live under the Torah (Father's household), he brings the true Mashiach with him (inside him), and the two sons become true brothers in Mashiach. These two houses are both only remnants, but they will be used to bring an uncountable number of lost Gentiles to the true faith, and obedience to Torah. This is to say that the false anti-Christ of the Christians will be exposed, perhaps the very "man of lawlessness", and people will understand in the last days. It's Yahushua's work, but he uses us to be His witnesses to what He is doing. The re-gathering is taking place now! The prodigal son is returning to the Father's Covenant.

WAS PAUL A HERETIC?

Considering Paul (Sha'ul), the Natsari Pharisee

There's a growing number of people debating over Sha'ul* these days. Generally, there are three views of him. Kepha (Peter) told us that Sha'ul's letters were difficult to understand (2Kepha 3:15,16), and his words were "twisted" by the untaught and unstable.

View #1: For the bulk of Christian history, Catholicism taught that salvation comes by receiving "grace" through "sacraments", and that any obedience to the Commandments of YHWH was seen as "*Judaizing*" and cut them off from Messiah. The Reformation started on the path back to the Truth by rejecting any salvation based on human efforts, such as "indulgences" or the "7 sacraments" - yet Luther still brought a few of the "sacraments" out with him! Sha'ul's writings have been used to defend the position that believers are saved by "grace alone" (Eph. 2:8,9). Sha'ul's so-called "anti-Torah" (anti-law) comments have been used mostly by the Reformers, because they desire to maintain the Replacement Theology of Romanism (that the "church" replaced Yisrael), setting aside any application of the Ten Commandments as having bearing on inheriting eternal life. The Ten Commandments that define sin have been annulled in this view, and salvation through belief in Yahushua's shed blood supercedes any need to obey. They claim we are now "free" from the "curse" of the law, and anyone attempting to obey the "Old Covenant" is seen as a heretic, Judaizer, and a reprobate. For centuries this view was enforced through the

Shaul - this is what Yahushua called the fellow we call "Paul" Acts 9:5

Catholic institution's dogmas as well, and any competing views were vigorously eliminated - with extreme prejudice (they were killed). It was a man named Marcion that promoted the forbidding of what is called the "Old Covenant", which included the Torah, the Prophets, and the Writings. He allowed only the writings of what came to be known as the "New Testament".

View #2: Today there are others who go to the other extreme, and call Sha'ul himself a heretic who was responsible for the "apostasy", the falling-away from the Torah by Christianity. For those who believe Sha'ul's letters indicated an annulling of any Commandments pertaining to the definition of sin, or that he contradicted the words of Rabbi Yahushua, please consider that you may have *misunderstood* what Sha'ul was referring to.

View #3: We who accept Sha'ul but reject "lawlessness" have been given a balanced understanding of his letters. Sha'ul was the apostle to the Gentiles, who were known as **adult male converts** "uncircumcised" *in their flesh.*

The letter to the Galatians (and other texts) addressed the "law" of adult male circumcision, which had been up to that time a cornerstone for any Gentile converting to the faith of Abraham, Yitshaq, and Ya'aqob. Further study will reveal this; even Kepha (Peter) pointed out that Shaul's letters were not easy to understand, but were "twisted" by those who were untaught (2 Kepha 3:15,16). Kepha warned us to watch, lest we be led away to destruction by the delusion of the lawless. He didn't include Sha'ul as a lawless one, but stated that Sha'ul's letters were being twisted, as were *"the other writings"*. For those who have interpreted that Sha'ul wrote of an "end of the law", Kepha's warning was written directly to those who live without the Torah! Those who live and believe they are "free" to disregard the Commandments are in spiritual danger; Kepha mentioned their "destruction" — so this is critical to get corrected (and why I'm writing this to you all!). For those who believe Sha'ul was a heretic that needs to be exposed for what he wrote about bringing an "end of the law", you have also misunderstood his writings. Kepha called Shaul "our beloved brother" at 2Kepha 3:15. Is Kepha a heretic also? Luke, who wrote about 40% of the Brith Chadasha (Re-newed Covenant, or Messianic Writings), was the most orderly writer of them all. He started at the beginning, writing both "Luke" and "Acts" to a person referred to as *"most excellent Theophilos"*. He began his first narrative with the birth of Yohanan, Yahushua's cousin. He tells us how Yohanan immersed Yahushua. Yohanan was finally imprisoned and beheaded by Herod. In chapter 3, Luke expounds the lineage of Yahushua, and goes on in the rest of his book to describe all the miracles and teachings of the Messiah of Yisrael. Luke also wrote the "Acts" of the apostles; and of no small mention is Sha'ul, the source of so much misunderstanding. Sha'ul is described as the *"apostle to the Gentiles"*, and Luke traveled with him to many cities witnessing in the synagogues. Luke recorded Sha'ul's conversion, and Yahushua didn't seem to think Shaul was a "heretic", but rather Yahushua Himself told HananYah of Sha'ul:

"Go, for he is a chosen vessel of Mine to bear My Name before nations, sovereigns, and the children of Yisrael". Acts 9:15. HananYah stood corrected, but at first he thought Sha'ul to be the most dangerous man on Earth. Sha'ul was also at the Yerushalayim Council, Acts 15. How do you feel about Sha'ul now? If you regard Sha'ul to be a heretic, then you will also have to trash Kepha and Luke. The only way to overcome the misunderstanding of Sha'ul's letters is by seeing that he was under constant criticism (in his time) over the topic of adult male circumcision *for converts*. Acts 15 addressed this controversial matter, and it should have put it to rest forever; but we know that even today there are those who wrestle with it, causing division in the Body of Messiah. When Sha'ul seems to be saying we are no longer "under the law", the "law" to which he is referring concerns adult male circumcision of converts. Ephesians 2:8,9 discusses "works" not saving us; but Sha'ul refers to those ceremonial "works" which we had formerly relied on -- animal sacrifices, circumcision, etc.,. -- certainly he never meant the annulment of the Ten Commandments, which we obey as the re-newed Covenant, promised to us at YermeYahu 31:31 to be written on our hearts. At Ephesians 2:10, the next verse, Sha'ul states that we were created in Messiah to perform good works, and implies that this is to obey the Ten Commandments:

"For we are His workmanship, created in Messiah Yahushua unto good works, which Elohim prepared before-

hand that we should walk in them." Eph. 2:10.

The word "them" refers to the good works prepared before-hand - the Ten Words, called the Covenant, the Ten Commandments — Hebrew: *ESRET HA'DABARIM.*

Works are the **fruit** of our faith, and perfect our belief.

Notice a few texts that discuss **works**:

*"Let your light so shine before men, that they may see your good **works** , and esteem your Father which is in Heaven."* Matt 5:16

*"For the Son of man shall come in the esteem of his Father with his angels; and then he shall reward every man according to his **works**."* Matt 16:27

*"Even so faith (belief), if it has not **works**, is dead, being alone. Yea, a man may say, you have faith, and I have works: show me your faith without your **works**, and I will show you my faith by my **works*** (the key to properly understanding obedience, and it's place in our lives). *You believe that there is one Elohim; you do well: the devils <u>also</u> believe, and tremble. But will you know, O vain man, that faith without **works** (obedience) is dead? Was not Abraham our father justified by **works**, when he had offered Yitshaq his son upon the altar? You see how faith worked through his **works** , and by **works** was faith made perfect?"* James 2:17-22

("Grace alone" through faith, without works, is moot -- "dead").

If we believe, but don't **obey** the Commandments, Yahushua will not be able to say "Well done" - but He will only be able to say "Well believed". Although "human effort" doesn't save us, when we are saved a great deal of "human effort" gets in line with the correct way of living. It is difficult for the elect (Matt 7:14, 1Pet. 4:18) -- but when you LOVE what you do because He has given you the **desire to obey** in your heart, it is not a grievous burden to obey the Commandments of YHWH — It's an act of love.

Ephesians 2:11,12 - These verses continue with awesome information. These reveal that Gentiles are <u>no longer</u> Gentiles when they are converted and immersed, but they become FELLOW CITIZENS of Yisrael (there's only ONE body with no division). So, please understand that the "uncircumcision" (in the flesh) are indeed circumcised, being

the *"workmanship of Yahushua"* - circumcised by Him in their hearts with a love for Torah.
(read Col. 2:11-13, Romans 2:28,29, 1 Cor. 7:19).

We are the **workmanship** of Yahushua, as we see at Ephesians 2:8-12, and this text explains that those "*formerly Gentile*" (they are no longer Gentile) called the "uncircumcision" by the "circumcision", are brought near through the blood of Mashiach - it isn't the circumcision made in the flesh by hands:

"Therefore remember that you, once Gentiles in the flesh, who are CALLED 'the uncircumcision' by what is CALLED 'the circumcision' made in the flesh by hands, that at that time you were without Messiah, excluded from the citizenship of Yisra'el and strangers from the covenants of promise, having no expectation and without Elohim in the world. But now in Messiah Yahushua you who once were far off have been brought near by the blood of the Messiah." Eph. 2:11-13

There are many other texts that show that "works" by *our hands* cannot save us - so even here Sha'ul is once again being misunderstood concerning obedience. He's referring to the *circumcision* made by the hands of men when he is talking about "works" not saving us.
(Remember: The CONTEXT reveals the meaning).

"By this we know that we love the children of Elohim, when we love Elohim, and keep His Commandments. For this is the love of Elohim, that we keep His Commandments: and his Commandments are not grievous." 1 John 5:2-3

"Think not that I am come to destroy the law, or the prophets: I am not come to destroy, but to fulfill. For verily I say unto you, till Heaven and Earth pass, one jot or one tittle shall in no wise pass from the law (Torah), till all be fulfilled. Whosoever therefore shall break one of these least Commandments, and shall teach men so, he shall be called the least in the kingdom of Heaven: but whosoever shall do and teach them, the same shall be called great in the kingdom of Heaven." Matt 5:17-19

At Revelation 2, Yahushua warned the *first* assembly that He would remove their *menorah* if they did not repent and do the "first works".   Repenting and obeying the **Torah**, many of us have received the symbol of the menorah, restored to us by Yahushua.   No man designed the menorah; it's design was provided by our Creator, given to Mosheh at Sinai.   The menorah is the symbol of Yahushua, the **Giver of the Torah**, the Word made flesh.   He is the "living Word", the Torah (teachings) come to life.   The parables are all pointing to one thing: the restoration of men to the Covenant relationship with YHWH.   Repent, and He will enable you to obey His Ten Commandments.   He will write them on your heart, and you will love His Torah.   He said:

"If you love Me, keep My Commandments."

His final warning to all the world:

"Repent, for the reign of YHWH draws near."

The Ten Commandments will be around for **all eternity**, and apply to every "mortal" being.   And, they also apply to every "immortal being" that has ever been created by YHWH.   The adversary seems to have a problem with obeying them, so it's easy to see why so many of us have been deceived - and deception is the main objective of our enemy.   Discerning Truth is a matter of how one looks at the Scriptures.   It's either with an "eye of light" or an "eye of darkness".   Sha'ul has been used to make people stumble, but only those who have an "eye of darkness".   The bottom line is, Sha'ul/Paul was endorsed by Rabbi Yahushua with these words:

"Go, for he is a chosen vessel of Mine to bear My Name before nations, sovereigns, and the children of Yisrael" - Acts 9:15.

The controversies around him and "the law" that he is referring to have divided the brothers since they were written.   Is it the "MORAL law", or the "CEREMONIAL law" that Yahushua completed for us?   The truthful answer to this question will go against 1950 years of false interpretations of Sha'ul's writings.   The need for animal sacrificing and circumcision of the new adult male converts is fulfilled now - in Yahushua's "work".   Some want to hold to adult male circumcision for converts so much, they refuse to have fellowship with those who understand Sha'ul differently.   They may as well sacrifice animals as well, because they don't understand Sha'ul's writings.   We are the workmanship of Yahushua, not the works of the hands of men, so our salvation is not based on anything men can do to "correct" our flesh, or wear on their heads. Those perishing have not received a love for the Truth (Torah, the Covenant), while those who have received this love for Torah from Yahushua obey the Covenant and have fellowship with YHWH, and with the brothers.

Volumes can be said against Sha'ul, but that little sentence quoted above stands forever as an endorsement of him that I cannot refute.

Be careful of those who promote hatred on the internet. They can poison our hearts with lies and turn us into propagators of their guile. Sha'ul is being attacked because the veil is being lifted on his words, and many people are finally understanding them. This understanding is uniting us, and the adversary is doing everything possible to quell this working of Yahushua's Spirit. But, Yahushua is going to win in the end.

Sha'ul / Paul was not a Roman Catholic, and neither was Luke or Kepha. They didn't play with "holy water", or have any relics. They didn't dispense "grace" by means of 7 sacraments. They taught the message of the government/kingdom of YHWH, and YHWH's Commandments as Yahushua told them to do. As for Sha'ul, remember that if you speak against his work, you may just be speaking against Yahushua's work, because Yahushua endorsed him.

If Catholicism / Christianity is a "hybrid" mixture of Paganism and the Natsari faith, *don't blame Sha'ul* - look at Marcion, Cyprian, Augustine, Origen, Eusebius, Ossius, and Constantine! Sha'ul literally suffered for the Name of Yahushua: he was stoned and assumed dead! This may have been the source of Sha'ul's "thorn", since being stoned can leave you in quite a damaged state. Go easy on him; have a heart!

Omnipresence of Yahushua ha Mashiach

Only Elohim can forgive sins. He will not give praise due to Him to another, Yesha Yahu 42:8. We can only pray to Elohim. Can we pray to Yahushua, and will He hear us?

This subject needs to be considered carefully - but we will not all be on the same page with it until He comes.

"See, He is coming with the clouds, and every eye shall

see Him, even they who pierced Him.   And all the tribes of the Earth shall mourn because of Him.   Yea, Amen.
"'I am the Alef and the Tau, Beginning and End', says YHWH 'Who is and Who was and Who is to come, the Almighty'".   Revelation 1:7,8.

Yahuchanon (John) turned to see Who was speaking.   It was Yahushua (Yahshua, Yahoshua), standing in the center of 7 lampstands, the **menorah**.   The phrase *'Who is and Who was and Who is to come'* happens to be the *definition* or *meaning* of the Hebrew word, **"YaHUaH"** (yod-hay-waw-hay).   It means existence in *all three* tenses, simultaneously. People have a fairly easy way of making one into three. They say it was impossible to put Humpty-Dumpty back together after he had fallen into pieces.   But YHWH is a real Being;   can we put Him back together, and not cause a war on Earth?

What shall we think about Yahushua?.   What sort of BEING is He?   Who can forgive sins?   Only Elohim YHWH, the Almighty (El Shaddai) surely.   The authority to forgive sins -- or atone for them -- must be seriously considered and kept in mind as we study this sensitive topic.   Since Yahushua came, there has been controversy among His students/followers regarding Who He is.   Yahushua raised the dead, and He also claims to have raised Himself:
"Destroy this Temple, and in three days I will raise it up."
Yn. (John) 2:19.   This may seem to be a conflict, but not if you understand Him, and Who He really is, and what the words might mean.   Galatians 1:1 states that Father YHWH raised Yahushua from the dead.   Titus 1:3 states that Elohim is our Savior, just as Yesha Yahu (Isaiah) 43 informs us.   The Torah is His Word, and the Scriptures themselves are about Him.   If you have Him (Messiah Yahushua), you have the Father also, so we see Scripture teaches.   Does that mean there are two persons involved, or just one?   If we don't solve the equation, no harm is done really.   This short study will take many components or hints from Scripture, and reduce them to their simplest form, and probably cause many to dispute back and forth over various texts and translations.   We will all wrestle with this until we are clothed with immortality, to be sure!   It should not divide us however.   There is a "Spirit" at work in believers, and this Spirit is Yahushua of Natsarith,

the Mashiach. There is a mystery concerning a knowledge of Messiah. Ephesians 1:17,18 tells us that our "*knowledge of Him*" (Messiah) is given to us by YHWH, as a Spirit of wisdom and of revelation in the knowledge of Him. Colossians 2:9-12 tells us:

"For in Him all the fullness of Deity dwells in bodily form, and in Him you have been made complete, and He is the head over all rule and authority; and in Him you were also circumcised with a circumcision made without hands, in the removal of the body of the flesh by the circumcision of Messiah, having been buried with Him in baptism (immersion), in which you were also raised with Him through faith in the working of Elohim, who raised Him from the dead."

So, the Messiah, Yahushua, is the Being Who indwells His people, and circumcises their hearts with a love for Torah, which is the promised Brit Chadasha (A circumcision is called a Brith, and this Hebrew word means "COVENANT", *to cut*). The preceding text says that Elohim raised Messiah from the dead; yet, we know that Yahushua said <u>HE</u> would raise Himself after 3 days. Who is Yahushua? Could He be El Shaddai, Elohim YHWH? At Rev. 1:8, Yahushua claims to be El Shaddai (the Almighty). He said *"I and My Father are one."* Yn. 10:30. The mystery, or secret, to be proclaimed among the Gentiles, is simply that *"Messiah is in you"* - Col. 1:27, Philippians 2:13, 2 Yn. v.9. This <u>requires</u> omnipresence. Other texts which declare this are at 2Cor. 13:5, Gal. 2:20, and Eph. 3:17. The **_Shema_** (Debarim 6:4) declares Elohim YHWH is <u>ONE</u>. If He were multiple personalities, we'd surely know. So, if there is only one Elohim, and that Elohim descended to become a man, and He told us that's what happened, why get tough with each other over it? Below, I will quote some texts that will make declarations concerning this topic, but there are many more.

If Yahushua is not in you, you are not His. 2 Cor. 13:5. Yahushua revealed the Father to mankind, and came to destroy the works of the devil. Through Yahushua, we come to (a knowledge of) the Father: *"I am the way, and the truth, and the life; no one comes to the Father, but through Me."* Yn. 14:6. If we know Yahushua, *then we also know the Father.*

"If you had known Me, you would have known My Father also; from now on you know Him, and have seen Him. Philip said to Him, "Master, show us the Father, and it is enough for us." Yahushua said to him, "Have I been so long with you, and yet you have not come to know Me, Philip? He who has seen Me has seen the Father; how do you say, 'Show us the Father?'" Yn. 14:6-9.

Mind-blowing! To get even a *slippery* handle on where any of this is headed, we all have to keep a very loose, open approach to how we think about this unique Being; and be careful about how we apply words to describe it all. It is easiest to simply think of Yahushua and YHWH as two Beings, and simply stop there before your head over-heats. And, no one is saying this is a problem; but if you want to press on, it will make you a little unusual. 2 Cor. 5:19 tells us Elohim was in Messiah, to reconcile us to Himself.

1Yn. chapter 3 discusses the operation of the Spirit in believers -- and this Spirit is *only given to those who obey Him* (Acts 5:32 -- Ruach ha Qodesh dwells in us). The Spirit comes in the Name of Who? Yahushua! Omnipresence is required in order to accomplish this. Yahushua told us that He is the "Life", and He said the comforter, the Ruach ha Qodesh, would be sent to guide us into all Truth. Yn. 6:63 tells us that it is the Spirit Who gives us Life (and this Spirit is the Spirit of Yahushua of course). 2 Tim. 1:14 tells us that this Spirit dwells in us, making the Spirit everywhere at once. Yahushua told us that He and His Father would come to us -- and live in us (Yn. 14:23). Two Beings? Perhaps just One Being, identified in two uniquely distinct ways. The Spirit was promised (Joel 2:32) and poured-out on the believers (Acts 2:38). There are many evidences provided in Scripture of the omnipresence (as well as omnitemporality and omnipotence) of YHWH's Spirit. Being temporal beings ourselves, we perceive things in simplistic ways, and can only understand partially at that. When Yahushua said **"the Father is greater than I"**, we immediately reconcile it by thinking of two Beings, and one is more than the other in power, scope, authority, and so on. That's fine. However, if we can accept it, by revelation in the knowledge of Him, "the Son" is the "container" which was brought into existence as a human form through which the Father (YHWH) manifested Himself to His creation. Sure, this is tough to deal with; and it's perfectly fine to struggle with -- I don't pretend to have my mind wrapped around it yet.   But, we must not judge one another over this kind of thing either.   To even begin to think about this "mental imaging" topic quickly shows all of us our limitations.   It's not important enough to argue over, but those who have been given a special Spirit of wisdom and of revelation in the knowledge of Him can appreciate what this article is really about.   The rest may find the topic heretical.

Emmanuel, Prince of Peace, Everlasting Father, Mighty Elohim   ~   these all refer to ONE Being; but there's much more to consider. At Revelation chapter 1 quoted above, we find the One speaking calling Himself *"the Almighty", the living One; and I was dead, and behold, I am alive forevermore"*. Fascinating. Micah, the prophet, at 5:2 tells us that Bethlehem Ephrathah would have One *"go forth for Me to be Ruler in Israel. His goings forth are from long ago, from the days of eternity."*   There is only one eternal Being, and He tells us there is no one beside Him, and identifies Himself as the first and the last   Yesha Yahu 41:4, 44:6.
"I, I am YHWH, and besides Me there is no Savior."
Yesha Yahu 43:11.

ZecharYah 14 tells us about the *return* of Yahushua to Earth;   the text describes the "Day of YHWH", and how YHWH will gather *"all the nations against Yerushaliyim to battle"*. *"Then YHWH will go forth and fight against those nations, as when He fights on a day of battle. And in that day His feet will stand on the Mount of Olives . . . and YHWH will be King over all the Earth; in that day YHWH will be the only one, and His name the only one."* Notice that this same event is described in chapter 12, and "the inhabitants" will recognize Him and mourn: v.10   *"And it will come about in that day that I will set about to destroy all the nations that come against Yerushaliyim. And I will pour out on the house of David and on the inhabitants of Yerushaliyim the Spirit of chen* (favor) *and supplication, so that they will look on Me whom they have pierced, and they will mourn for Him as one mourns for an only son, and they will weep bitterly over Him, like the bitter weeping over a first-born."*

The omnipresence of Yahushua (the Spirit of Yahushua) is

seen in how He healed the synagogue ruler's daughter from a distance. He didn't need the address, but already knew all about the man and his family. He knew when His friend Lazarus was sick, and the moment he died. Even with the internet and cell phones, no normal person or being can know and do the things Yahushua accomplished. Limiting Yahushua and His abilities in our eyes can quickly lead to questioning other matters concerning Him, and new doubts may ultimately lead to a loss of faith in Who He is, and what He accomplished. Teaching others to think of Yahushua as being simply a special man means we have to become blind to many, many Scriptures which indicate otherwise. Yahushua is one of 3 possible things: Master, liar, or lunatic. His actions confirm He is Elohim -- without them we may be able to suspect Him of being deluded, or a liar. When we stand before Him, we will know and sense better Who He really is; He will shake the heavens with His voice at His return, not just the Earth. We are puny creatures incapable of creating life; He is the Author of it.

Notice this phrase carefully: *". . . whatever you ask of the Father in My Name, He might give you."* Yn. 15:16. Then, at Yn. 16:25, Yahushua explains, *"These things I have spoken to you in figurative language; an hour is coming when I will speak no more to you in figurative language, but will tell you plainly of the Father."* Yahushua is holding back a great deal, so of course we currently dispute each other's understandings of His true identity and relationship to Father YHWH. *"All things that the Father has are Mine; therefore I said that He takes of Mine, and will disclose it to you."* Yn. 16:15. The fact is, Yahushua is the One, and the Source, from which and by which our prayers are answered: *"If you ask whatever in My Name I shall do it."* Yn. 14:14. The more you study about this, the more your point of view will differ from those who haven't studied it.

All things that are the Father's are Yahushua's (and this includes His abilities), Yn. 15:16. Creatures cannot raise the dead, nor create anything. The authority to forgive sins rests solely with Yahushua, and He will be the Judge of the living and the dead. Yahushua raised Lazarus and others from the dead, and His Spirit in the talmidim raised the dead and healed the sick and lame. In Yahushua's Name there is found the forgiveness of sins, the power of healing, and authority over demonic spirits. It would seem that Yahushua is a "role" (a function or position) through which Father YHWH manifests Himself to His creation. Of course when we only superficially survey the various statements made such as *"the Father is greater than I"*, we can still be missing the point Yahushua is trying to convey to us. To the men seeing and hearing Yahushua at that time, the Person of Yahushua standing before them certainly was "lesser" in every sense of the word than Father YHWH. He had humbled Himself infinitely to take on the form of men. His rank was below that of the messengers (Hebrews 2:7); and He came into the world He had created. *"He was in the world, and the world came to be through Him, and the world did not know Him. He came to His own, and His own did not receive Him."* Yn. 1:10,11. YHWH exists not only throughout infinite space, but also time -- infinity past and future. He's actually there in time. It is laid bare before Him every nanosecond. Every moment of all time is His reality. One million years in our future timeline doesn't exist for us, as temporal beings. But, YHWH is there right now. His goings-forth are from eternity. He doesn't just KNOW the future, or the past, He is there at all times, holding all things together. He knows your innermost thoughts, and He created the spirit within you that makes you uniquely you. His powers are unfathomable. His Name, YHWH actually means *"I was, I am, and I will be"*, or *'Who is and Who was and Who is to come'*. He is THE Eternal Being, but He hides Himself; only those diligently seeking will find Him. These same "diligent seekers" have to take some great risks -- in other words, they are not lacking in courage. He made them that way. But, He dislikes the cowardly, or those who faint away and won't bear up under the scorn of man. We must endure our "thorns" -- those who would make it their occupation to torture us for our courage and faithfulness.

Some believe it is wrong to "_worship_" Yahushua; yet Hebrews 1:6 tells us the messengers (angels) worship Him. Messengers are on record in Scripture saying to various men that we are to only worship YHWH. In spite of all the hints in Scripture, people resist making it all add up. The hints are like the components in a big equation, but people often will not solve the equation, because it will make Yahushua equal to YHWH, and reveal that "they" are in fact "ONE" -- exactly as it should be. When ha shatan tempted Yahushua in the wilderness, Yahushua responded to it in an interesting way: *"You shall not try* (test) *YHWH your Elohim".* Mt. 4:7. Imagine any creature making a statement like that -- including an "angel". It would be blasphemous for any creature to make such a statement. Remember, angels (messengers, or malakim) are creatures too ~ they were simply created before the Earth, and the first man, Adam. Malakim were not designed to ever terminate, or stop living, so they aren't *"mortal"* (from the Hebrew muth, and Latin mort, for death).

The Spirit of Truth comes in the Name of Yahushua, and Yahushua is the Truth and the Life. Messiah is to be *All in all* (Col. 3:11); the objective of YHWH is to be *All in all* (1 Cor. 15:28). YHWH and Yahushua are One, not two or three. Yahushua is an aspect of YHWH, revealing the Father to us. Many try to make "them" into a "twinity" or "trinity", but these teachings originate from outside Scripture. When the day arrives and we stand before Yahushua, we can ask Him to show us the Father. He may have the same answer for us that He did for brother Philip, and that will be enough for me. Yahushua's omnipresence is one of the main problems for ha shatan. One of the first realizations I had when I was a child was that Yahushua is omnipresent, and that I could talk to Him. Praying to the dead is an abomination, and quite silly. The Catholics across the whole Earth pray to "Mary". There are 3 obstacles to her hearing their prayers:
1. She's not omnipresent;
2. She doesn't speak any language but Hebrew (or the dialect of it called Aramaic), so she can't understand a word they are saying;
3. She's dead. Yahushua can hear us, He is everywhere (in the universe), and He's alive. See the subtle distinctions there? If we found ourselves in space beyond the visible galaxies, He would still be there with us. Even if much of this is a huge misunderstanding on my part, at least Messiah is preached; see Philippians 1:12-30.

Philippians 2:5-8 tells us that Elohim YHWH took the form of a bond-servant, being made in the likeness of men. Verse 11 is the clincher. Philippians 2:13,14 tells us that it is Elohim Who is working in you -- and that we should be without grumblings and disputings, in order to be blameless, to shine as lights in the world amid a perverse generation. If Elohim is in us, and the Messiah is in us, then we know more about Who Messiah is. No creature can ride two chariots (or cars) at the same time, or ride two horses; yet Messiah is in many of us right now. He's no created being, He's the Creator.

"And He is the image of the invisible Elohim, the first-born of all creation. For by Him all things were created, both in the heavens and on Earth, visible and invisible, whether thrones or dominions or rulers or authorities -- all things have been created by Him and for Him. And He is before (foremost) all things, and in Him all things hold together. He is also head of the Body, the ekklesia (Hebrew, qahal), and He is the beginning, the first-born from the dead; so that He Himself might come to have first place in everything. For it was the Father's good pleasure for all the fulness to dwell in Him, and through Him to reconcile all things to Himself, having made peace through the blood of His stake; through Him, I say, whether things on Earth or things in heaven."
Colossians 1:16-20

When the day arrives that the Children of YHWH are revealed to the universe, and Yahushua takes the Throne, He will be the Sovereign of sovereigns, and Master of masters (Rev. 19). *"For let this mind be in you which was also in Messiah Yahushua, Who being in the form of Elohim, did not regard equality with Elohim a matter to be grasped, but emptied Himself, taking the form of a servant, and came to be in the likeness of men."* Philippians 2:5-7. *"Elohim, therefore, has highly exalted Him and given Him the Name which is above every name, that at the Name of Yahushua every knee should bow, of those in heaven, and of those on Earth, and of those under the Earth, and every tongue should confess that Yahushua is Master, to the esteem of Elohim the Father."* Philippians 2:9-11.

If Yahushua _is_ Elohim, as I believe He is, we may worship Him and pray to Him; and whatever we ask in His Name, He will do it. This is to say we have to be asking in HIS will, since He gives us the desire (in our hearts) to ask for the things; He will not give us whatever WE want). Let Elohim YHWH be the Judge of these conclusions, and let me fall into His forgiving hands -- but let me not fall into the hands of men. It is not for everyone to understand this, and it is certainly not a salvational issue. If this study leans away from what traditional human doctrines have established, such as the Nicene Creed or Apostle's Creed (both Catholic conventions), all well and good. In the fullness of time, it will be revealed to us all -- ***"But let Elohim be true, and every man a liar, as it has been written, 'That you should be declared right in Your words, and prevail in Your judging.'"*** Romans 3:4.

If I didn't use enough Scripture, please let me know. If there were just a couple of places in Scripture that suggested that Yahushua is Elohim, one might suspect there could be some misunderstanding. Many folks can justify believing in the doctrine of the "trinity" -- having only a few proof-texts to hang on (and being in conflict with many other texts), but the above Scriptural texts are not *"proof-texts"*, but they actually teach the conclusions this article addresses. The Savior, or Mashiach, seems to be equivalent *in every way* to YHWH. For example, YHWH claims He is the King (Melek) of Israel, but at the same time we find that Yahushua is also. YHWH is the "husband" of Israel, and yet Yahushua is the *"Bridegroom"*. He's not the best-man, or number 2 in any way. They merge together into One, if you follow everything to its logical conclusion. The arguments against these conclusions are usually based on deriving radically different interpretations of the text, and I'm not implying they are in error -- they are simply radically different interpretations. Also, in order to arrive at certain interpretations, it may be claimed that specific articles were mistranslated, leading one to arrive at the wrong conclusion. Another explanation that some people give is that the Brit Chadasha (Messianic Writings, or Renewed Covenant Writings) have been tampered with, and certain ideas were added to "deify" Yahushua. I like to use the "Ockham's Razor" approach, and keep it as simple as possible. Let there be no striving and fighting among us -- Mashiach is proclaimed, and that is what is most important. To some of us, He is simply more important than anything else.

Ockham's Razor: After *William of Ockham + RAZOR*
(as a sharp instrument for cutting away non-essentials).
A principle in science and philosophy urging the use of the most economical and least complex assumptions, terms, and theories and stating that an explanation for unknown phenomena should first be attempted in terms of what is already known. It is usually formulated as:

"Entities should not be multiplied unnecessarily."

A Revelation straight from the pages of Scripture:

IS THE WRITER OF REVELATION STILL ALIVE?

Yochanan was exiled to the island of Patmos in the Mediterranean Sea, where he was left to live out the rest of his mortal life. While most Christians have been taught that he was seeing and hearing incorporeal, ephemeral-visions on a "Sun-day", *the truth of the matter is quite different.* The statement, *"I was in the Spirit on the Lord's day"* (as we often see it translated) is really telling us that he was *spiritually transported to the future "Day of YAHUAH"*, a period of time we may better understand as being the "great tribulation", ending in the return of Yahushua haMashiach with all of His resurrected set-apart ones, His bride- Yisrael. **Time periods** are the main theme in this "revelation", and they are intentionally written for, and to those set-apart ones of Israel who are living through the time periods, so they will recognize the events being revealed by Yahushua, the Revelator. So, "day" refers to the **period of time** at the end of days, not a specific day of the week. Certainly, the "Lord's Day" is never used in Scripture to refer to the day of the week called "Sun-day," which human tradition has led us to believe is now the Sabbath. To believe this could be so is caused by the **mesmerization** of the masses.   Just as we might arrange a "conference call" on a telephone, Yahushua can *"time-patch"* reality as He did at Mt. 17:1-3, when He transformed and shone like the sun, talking with Mosheh and Eliyahu. Likewise, brother Yochanan was "time-patched" forward to the great, awesome, and dreadful Day of YAHUAH. It is from this book, **Chizayon** (Revelation), that we learn there will be **"2 witnesses"** who will prophesy in the last days. Yochanan reports to us that _he_ was told:

    "You have to <u>prophesy again</u> concerning many people and nations and sovereigns" at chapter 10:11.
~ _Could he be one of these <u>two</u> <u>witnesses</u>?_

Did Yochanan die on Patmos? Traditional records tell us he was boiled in oil _three times_; obviously he had been accused of a capital crime — and if they couldn't put him to death, it helps explain why he was **exiled** to Patmos. Is there any _Scriptural evidence_ to support the possibility that the author of this book may be STILL ALIVE? Well, in fact, YES THERE IS. One clue is given at Mt. 16:27,28, where Yahushua speaks of the time of His return, then mentions something very curious:

"For the Son of Adam is going to come in the esteem of His Father with His messengers, and then He shall reward each according to his works. Truly, I say to you, there are some <u>standing here</u> who shall <u>not taste death</u> at all until they see the Son of Adam coming in His reign."

At Yn. 21:18, Yahushua tells Kepha what kind of **death** he will have to endure, then Kepha asks Yahushua about Yochanan concerning this same topic, his death. Yn. 21:20
"And now Kepha, turning around, saw the taught one whom Yahushua loved following, who also had leaned on His breast at the supper, and said, 'Master, who is the one who is delivering You up?' Seeing him, Kepha said to Yahushua, 'But Master, what about this one?' _(Referring to Yochanan's death)_
Yahushua said to him, 'If I wish him to remain until I come, what is that to you?'"
"Therefore this word went out among the brothers that this taught one would not die." - 21:23. But, Yochanan went on to clarify that Yahushua didn't say he wouldn't die, but rather said **"If I wish him to remain until I come, what is that to you?"** So, he will die eventually - that is appointed for all men . . . but something special has been arranged for Yochanan apparently!
So let's watch, pray, and keep the book of Revelation continually part of our study and research.
"Blessed is he who reads and those who hear the words of this prophecy, and guard what is written in it, for the time is near." _Chizayon_ (Revelation) 1:3

GALL: IMPUDENCE, EFFRONTERY — IN CASE YOU DIDN'T KNOW, I'M ONLY JESTING HERE. BY ALL MEANS, TEACH!

Near is the Day of YAHUAH, and the 2 witnesses.

THE JUDAIZERS

We all know that Shaul (Paul) clearly told us that prior to the coming of Messiah Yahushua and our gathering together to Him there would be a *"falling away"* first, and the *"man of lawlessness"* would be revealed. He even referred to the coming of Yahushua as *"the day of Yahuah"* (2 Thess. 2:1-17). The "falling away" refers to a religious movement AWAY from the **Commandments** of Yahuah, also known as the "apostasy". Lawlessness will be promoted prior to the *"day of Yahuah"*. Understand, this *"day of Yahuah"* will only end the *"times of the Gentiles"*, and it will establish a government (kingdom) on this Earth that will grow and fill it completely, never to end. It will be ruled by the coming King, Yahushua of Natsarith, seated on the rebuilt throne of Da'ud! The Ten Commandments are intended for all men who enter into the everlasting Covenant with their Maker, and when they do this they become **citizens of Israel**. They were "far off", but now they are brought near, and have fellowship with one another, and with their Creator, the One Who gave the Covenant. Notice this statement carefully:

"Now all has been heard; here is the conclusion of the matter : Fear Elohim and keep His Commandments, for this is the whole [duty] of man. For Elohim will bring every deed into judgment, including every hidden thing, whether it is good or evil." Eccl 12:13-14

The Commandments aren't exclusive to the "Jews", in fact "Jews" are no longer Israelites if they do not keep the Commandments - they are CUT OFF from Israel. The **engrafted** foreigners partake of all the promises, and have eternal life, and are **no longer foreigners**. The are no longer Gentiles (Eph. 2:11-13). They are "formerly Gentiles". Turning themselves around, or "repenting" of sinning against the Covenant, their hearts have changed, and their will is to serve and obey Yahuah (read Is. 56). Those who have not received a LOVE for the Commandments, but rather repel them and teach others to repel them, have received a strong delusion to believe in the lie. Those that have accepted Yahushua's death as atonement, and entered the Covenant through the waters of immersion have been "circumcised" with a love of the Covenant, the Ten Commandments - by the Messiah, Yahushua! Men have twisted many things. Without the Light of Torah, most lack Wisdom, Understanding, and Knowledge, which is what the Ten Commandments would give them.

Here is an example of apostasy: During the 4th century, the Roman Emperor Constantine I "decreed" the _"Edict of Constantine"_ (321 CE), causing every citizen to REST on the Pagan's day of worship, the "Day of the Sun", now called "Sun Day". They were sun worshippers, and this edict was enforced under penalty of death. Just a few years later, at the "Council of Nicea" (325 CE), he and his son Crispus set up the "Universal" (Catholic) date to observe for "Easter", a fertility rite of the Earth Mother, Ishtar. He had called Natsarim elders to this "Council", and many of them fled for their lives. Sun-day was established as the "Sabbath", and it has continued to this day in the minds of those under the influence of this "strong delusion". Now you may be seeing a glimpse of light coming on as you realize that one man imposed this "change" of the "times and law", referred to at Daniel 7:25.

Over the centuries, the religiously powerful rulers of the Catholic institution have carried on this delusion, and it crossed-over into the Reformation just a few hundred years ago. All during the Catholic/Universal tyranny that gripped Europe during the Dark Ages, the "Jewish" faith was severely persecuted. They (the Jews, or "Yahudim") were faced with the choice of flee, convert, or die. Being highly intelligent, educated people, the Yahudim often agreed to convert to Catholicism, and follow its plan of "salvation" through the "sacraments" administered through the Catholic "priesthood". These Yahudim converts were called "marranos", which meant "swine" or "filthy" to the Catholic institution (because they do not eat pork). They were considered "Neo-Christians". The Inquisition considered them to be heretics, and burned many of them at the stake. In contrast, we see that the record at Acts 15 not only endorses the original Sabbath Day, but encouraged the Gentile converts to learn more in the places of study, called "synagogues" throughout the world:

"For Mosheh of old time has in every city them that preach him, being read in the synagogue every Sabbath

day." This was speaking of "Mosheh" in the sense of the TORAH, and can generally apply to the first 5 books; but TO-RAH is also what YHWH calls His TEN Commands. But, note well that Ya'aqob (James) referred to that "dreaded" word, "*SABBATH*" in his statement. Whoa - perhaps even Ya'aqob would be considered one of those "Judaizers" by today's Christians for talking about the Sabbath the way he did.

Before the Hekal (Temple) was destroyed in 70 CE, to "Judaize" referred mostly to the teaching that ADULT males had to be physically circumcised in their flesh in order to be saved, or to fellowship with other Natsarim. Shaul cleaned Kepha's clock over this kind of attitude. We can read about this correction at Galatians 2:14:

"But when I saw that they walked not uprightly according to the truth of the gospel, I said unto Peter before them all, If thou, being a Jew, livest after the manner of Gentiles, and not as do the Jews, why compellest thou the Gentiles to live as do the Jews?" (Some translations use the word "Judaize" in this passage, however the word "Judaize" was not invented until the 16th century). In Shaul's time, many adult Gentile converts (those called to obey the Ten Commandments) were being compelled to be physically circumcised, when all they had to do was be immersed into the Name of Yahushua! He circumcises our HEARTS with His Covenant, the Ten Commandments, and our immersion in water is the outward sign of our circumcision of the heart- by Mashiach Yahushua. Although there are still some who teach adult male circumcision, this has thankfully been exposed by Scripture to be wrong. Today, a "Judaizer" is what you may be called *if you want to keep the Ten Commandments*! (We should, of course, see that our newly born male children are circumcised on the eighth day after their birth. Acts 15 and many of Shaul's letters explain that adult males need only to be immersed into Yahushua's Name.)

The world of Christian theology, both Catholic and Protestant, has coined the word "**Judaizers**" to label those who secretly or openly observe the original Sabbath day as given in the Ten Commandments. It follows that those who hate the Ten Commandments would also hate those who observe them, and so this derogatory term, "Judaizers", is used to denigrate anyone who would be so *"filthy"* as to actually **obey** the Commandment to rest on the 7th day of every week instead of the _1st_ day of the week (as most good Christians believe is the Sabbath). Imagine anyone with the unmitigated gall to actually *OBEY* the Commandments, and to *TEACH* them to other people! Wisdom is the word used as a metaphor for the Ten Commandments in the book of Proverbs, and all who hate Wisdom, love death. We see in the book of Revelation (12:17) that the dragon (serpent) was enraged at the "woman" (Israel, Yahuah's wife) and fights against her seed, *"those guarding the Commands of Elohim **AND** possessing the witness of Yahushua Mashiach."* (It's interesting that the 10 Commandments were called "the WITNESS" -- as in the "Ark of the Witness")

The Catholics are told that when Yahushua referred to the "keys" of His kingdom/government, that it was conferred on Kepha/Peter alone to personally decide what could be bound or loosed. This is far from the intention of Yahushua! He wasn't giving Kepha the keys to His sports car. Yahushua remains *"Master of the Sabbath",* not Kepha, or any "successor" we may believe to exist. What He intended for us to realize is that when we have ALL learned and practiced the Ten Commandments, we will understand them and love them with His enabling Spirit (He circumcises our hearts with a love for them, which is the re-newed Covenant prophesied at YermeYahu 31). Knowing them, we can "bind" (forbid) and "loose" (permit) behavior, knowing wrong and right. The Ten Commandments are the "eternal Covenant", and the character of Yahuah. These "Ten Words" are known as Torah in Hebrew, meaning "teaching". "I will give you the keys of the kingdom of heaven; whatever you bind on earth will be bound in heaven, and whatever you loose on earth will be loosed in heaven." Matt 16:19-20. These "keys", the Ten Commandments, define what is a sin for us, and give us power (authority) over every kind of evil. These keys lock and unlock, or bind and loose, open and close; determining evil and righteousness for us. He "gives" us the keys by writing them on our hearts. The Torah is also commonly called "law" by translators: *"Everyone who sins breaks the law; in fact, sin is lawlessness.* 1 Yn. 3:4

If we are called "Judaizers", then we are being accused of

obeying the Torah of Yahuah, particularly His Sabbath of rest. The modern term for us is "legalists". We obey because we love Him. If we were really "illegalists", then we would have the wrath of Yahuah abiding on our heads. Without the Ten Words, we would not be able to determine what a sin is!

Imagine for a moment you are standing before Yahushua, meeting Him for the first time. Suddenly angry shouting comes from behind you in the distance, saying:

"This person claimed to obey the Ten Commandments, and even went so far as to teach many others those Ten Commandments! This person is a LEGALIST!"

Wouldn't that be just *great*?

Question: What is the primary reason the denominations don't have fellowship with one another?

Answer: **They do not observe the Ten Commandments**. Most have been taught that to obey them is to attempt to trust in them for salvation; but this is a lie. We obey them BECAUSE we are saved, and because Yahushua has written them on our hearts.

If we don't have fellowship with one another, then we aren't "tuned" correctly. When everyone allows Yahuah's Covenant to be written on their hearts by Yahushua, and they receive a love for the Truth, then we can have fellowship with Him, and with one another. We cannot claim to have fellowship with Yahuah and at the same time disobey His Commandments. The false teachers can be identified by this criteria, whether or not they observe and teach Torah.

A NOTE ABOUT THOSE "*KEYS*":

He "gives" us the **keys** by writing them on our hearts.

ESART HA DEBARIM = THE TEN WORDS

Get yourself in tune by studying and memorizing the 10 Commandments. Da'ud said that he had memorized them:

"I have hidden your Word in my heart that I might not sin against you .
Praise be to you, Yahuah; teach me your decrees.
With my lips I recount all the laws that come from your mouth.
I rejoice in following your statutes as one rejoices in great riches.
I meditate on your precepts and consider your ways.

I delight in your decrees; I will not neglect your Word."
Ps 119:11-16   ("Word" = Torah)

"He that has My Mitzvot, and keeps them, he it is that loves Me;   and he who loves Me, shall be loved by My Abba, and I will love him, and will reveal Myself to him."
Yochanon 14:21

"And pray that your flight does not take place in winter or on the Sabbath." MattithYahu 24:20
(This statement was made concerning the conditions in the *end of days!).*   There's going to be a test; we can look for the *evidence* in those who are saved:

"And by this we know that we have come to know Him, if we keep His Commandments. The one who says, 'I have come to know Him,' and does not keep His Commandments, is a liar, and the Truth is not in him; but whoever keeps His Word, in him the love of Elohim has truly been perfected. By this we know that we are in Him: the one who says he abides in Him ought himself to walk in the same manner as He walked."   1 Yochanan 2:3-6

Author's Response to Two Critics of the Fossilized Customs book

The following comments are from a congregational leader in Texas, and another person who consulted her pastor concerning various topics.   Following each disputed issue, I briefly address the situation point-by-point - and I'll tell you in advance that I don't take the "traditional" position.   There are certain congregational leaders who seem to take opposition with some of these same topics discussed in Fossilized Customs.

(Lew's opening comments):

If a member of the Body is found to be practicing or teaching error, he is to be confronted by the offended person privately first, and if this fails it is to be brought before the elders. If this fails to correct the man's error, it is to be brought before the whole assembly of saints, so that his shame is before all (Mt. 18:15-17). If I am a false witness to some, then I am in good company; Sha'ul was thought to be one because he witnessed that Elohim raised up Messiah (1 Cor. 15:15) -- a very unpopular idea to the establishment. To the establishment,   men   who   expose   error   have   usually and understandably been labeled rebels, or worse.   As Sha'ul stated at Philippians 1:15-18, he rejoiced in the fact that Messiah was announced, whether in pretense, envy, strife, or selfish ambition -- so in the spirit of this concept I will not speak against anyone who is working in the harvest and giving of themselves in Yahushua's service.   In the criticisms that follow, I find no circumstances which effect one's salvation before YHWH, regardless of which way one leans in belief.   It would be my privilege to respond briefly to these sincere concerns regarding what is found to be offensive in my book Fossilized Customs, but I do not hope to win a debate at the expense of offending or shaming my brothers and sisters:

Response to First Critic:

congregational leader: "In the Oct-Dec 2003 issue of Petah Tikvah, on page 4, you have footnote 2, which makes mention of "Fossilized Customs" by Lew White. Let me make you aware of the dangerous material contained within this book. Lew White does not believe in the Tri-unity of the Godhead. He believes it's pagan in origin and based on pagan sexual practices (p. 91-93). "

Lew's response: If a person were to only have contact with the Scriptures, without any outside teachings or influences, it would be highly unlikely for them to develop a belief in a "Trinity" on their own. Too many texts reveal that YHWH is one, not three. *Exegesis* (direct analysis or interpretation of Scripture) will often conflict with what a person has been taught or already believes as he brings them with him to the study -- prior beliefs must not be allowed to influence such analysis. When we approach Scripture with ideas we already believe and then hunt down the texts which support our belief, we find ourselves "proof-texting". In this case, if we read a text, the teaching we already believe is not directly being taught, but we can snatch or extract the necessary phrases in order to support our belief. This is not exegesis, but rather eisegesis. *Eisegesis* (analyzing from one's own ideas) is what we mostly see being done, where an explanation or analysis is based upon one's own ideas, which is often based on popular opinion. Eisegesis (analyzing from one's own ideas) is what we mostly see being done, where an explanation or analysis is based upon one's own ideas, which is often based on popular opinion. Eisegesis (analyzing from one's own ideas) is what we mostly see being done, where an explanation or analysis is based upon one's own ideas, which is often based on popular opinion.

The "Trinity" entered the belief through what is called The Apostles' Creed, formulated as an integral part of the rite of baptism. A clearly divided and separate confession of Father, Son, and Holy Ghost, corresponding to the Divine Persons invoked in the formula of baptism was imposed by Catholicism, and this dogma has persisted strongly to the present. This Creed developed from a primitive teaching (c. 390), and is referred to in a letter addressed to Siricius by the Council of Milan (Migne, P.L., XVI, 1213), which supplies the earliest known instance of the combination Symbolum Apostolorum ("Creed of the Apostles"). Certainly any idea that it actually originated with the 12 Apostles is a myth. The actual inception of the doctrine of the Trinity seems to be best explained as coming from the Nicene Creed, formulated under the Emperor Constantine in 325 AD. All we need to do is find a text in the Scriptures which teaches anything about YHWH being three distinct persons, and that belief in such a model is so paramount that our salvation hangs on it. He is neither trinity or "twin-ity", but if we would condemn one another over whether He is or isn't, we are operating outside the bounds of what Scripture teaches us -- especially about judging one another. What I am guilty of (hopefully) is not judging people, but rather beliefs which entered the faith from outside. Constantine was marvelously talented at modifying and formulating things that appealed to what everyone already believed. He did not emphasize Scripture as our model and guide for doctrine. Fossilized Customs is not the only book which has been written which teaches that YHWH is one.

Sir Isaac Newton and Alexander Hislop were non-trinitarians. "In the unity of that one Only God of the Babylonians, there were three persons, and to symbolize that doctrine of the Trinity, they employed, as the discoveries of Layard prove, the equilateral triangle, just as it is well known the Romish Church does at this day. In both cases such a comparison is most degrading to the King Eternal, and is fitted utterly to pervert the minds of those who contemplate it, as if there was or could be any similitude between such a figure and Him Who hath said, 'To whom will you liken (Elohim), and what likeness will you compare unto Him?'" The Two Babylons, pgs. 16,17.

congregational leader: "He does not believe in the tithe and states it is a social decision and not a biblical commandment (p. 89)."

Lew's response: Anyone who has read Fossilized Customs can see that I cite many Scriptures which show that we are to tithe; the only controversy is *who is to be the recipient of it*. Yahushua was not supported by the tithe, but rather by those who were in the office of giving -- women of means (Luke 8:3, Mark 15:41). Miriam of Magdala was one of these women! The tithe is for the support of the widow, fatherless, lame, hungry, or any who are in temporary or permanent need of support. Giving to the poor is lending to YHWH (Proverbs 19:17, Ya'aqob 1:27, Acts 10:4). There are many examples in Fossilized Customs supporting the tithe, but I also cite several Scriptures which expose how the sheep will be fleeced for gain (2 Cor. 2:17, 2 Kepha 2:3, Acts 20:32-35). We who labor in teaching are worthy of support, but only from those in the office of "helps" (1 Cor. 12:28). No where do we see any leader in Scripture teaching his students to give him 10% of their income. Certainly no Apostle ever took such plunder for personal use from any assembly they started. Performing a study of the phrase "ravenous wolves" might shed light on this subject better. If you have the means to support a leader who is working in the service of Yahushua's Body, PLEASE do so; but to call it the tithe is inappropriate. For this teaching, I am willing to be shamed for; but let Yahushua judge me. He is so much more forgiving than men are. Those who oppose this teaching may have much to lose financially, but it is so much more blessed to give than to receive. I know, because I must receive to do the work I do also. Without support, I would not be enabled to do the work I do. Another good word to study in this context is "nicolaitan" (no offense to my critic intended).

congregational leader: "He believes ministers should not receive of tithes and offerings for their support. He believes ministers should get a job like everyone else and stop "bilking" the people out of their money."

Lew's response: Did Kepha have a job? Andrew, Kepha, and Yohanan did quite a bit of fishing, and not for sport. Paul was a maker of tents, and he mourned for the occasions he was supported by assemblies when he needed to impose on them (in his travels). He surely didn't confuse this support with the tithe; he carried offerings of food to the saints in Yerushaliyim when there was a famine (1 Cor. 16:3, Romans 15:26,27). The poor were *foremost* on the minds of these men (Galatians 2:10). We are to be supported as elders in the Body, and this is to do the work of the workman; we must not become a burden on every person to the extent of taking 10% from everyone's wages. Those with the means will have it put on their heart *to invest in our work*, and by doing so share in the rewards - our works become theirs also. Yahushua will reward each according to their WORKS (Mt. 16:27,28). The former Gentiles who reaped spiritually from the people of Elohim, the Yahudim / Israel, were encouraged to share materially with them (Romans 15:26,27). Our brother's word "offerings" above was never a topic I taught against in the book. I still feel that we who serve the Body should work in an auxiliary capacity to earn a living, *since we are not Levites and exempt from having a livelihood*. Each one of the Body is of the priesthood of Melckizedek, and we are the living stones of the Temple of YHWH.

congregational leader: "He does not believe in gathering on the Sabbath, or in fact, ever needing to gather as Believers."

Lew's response: We worship YHWH by our obedience every day. Gathering on Shabbat (or **after** Shabbat, as we see done in a home at Acts 20:7-12) is encouraged if possible in Fossilized Customs. But, we must study to see if it is **required** to assemble ON Shabbat for everyone, or not. Reading Exodus/Shemoth 16:29,30, we know we must not leave our "vicinity" on a Shabbat. Primarily, we are commanded to **assemble** 3 times in a year (males over 20). On a typical Shabbat, those who study *may do so* in their homes today with their families, where the basic focus or center of our life and walk begins. And there's nothing wrong with having an assembly on Shabbat, or any other day of the week. The small synagogues we read about in Scripture describe study groups of converting Gentiles, and native Israelites that wished to further their knowledge, or become teachers (rabbis) themselves. Yahuah told *parents* to teach His Torah to their children, no one else. We do not live to assemble; but we are to live to teach our children the Torah of YHWH. The small synagogues could never have contained all the Israelites in a town. In fact, Yahuah never commanded that synagogues even be built. When we assemble it is for edification, and here *each one* is to have a turn at teaching, prophesying, interpreting, revelations, singing, according to their gifts (1 Cor. 14:26). If we **never gather** together, the Voice of Yahushua cannot speak to the body -- the Spirit of prophecy is the testimony of Yahushua. He is in us, and teaches us **through** one another -- even the least of us. Perhaps our brother misunderstood what I meant in the book; we are not "obliged" or commanded to assemble each and every Shabbat (as Catholicism has taught for centuries about their Sunday worship services called the mass). If we choose to, we can sleep all day on Shabbat, and no wrong is done. Leaders who insist otherwise may have an agenda to push -- and their congregation should investigate what that may be. If a leader takes up a collection of **money** on the **Sabbath**, then they need to find where this behavior is seen in Scripture -- we should not be carrying money around at all on a Shabbat; even the beggars have to take this day off. What does this text mean: ***"Six days work is done, but the seventh day is a Sabbath of rest, a set-apart MIQRA.***

You do no work, it is a Sabbath to YHWH in all your dwellings." Please look up the Hebrew meaning of MIQRA, as it pertains to its root, **QARA**. The root meaning is *proclaim*, not *gather* or *convocate* as translators have rendered it.

congregational leader: "He believes in the 'Two House / Covenant' theory, whereas, all Gentiles Believers are descended from the lost 10 tribes of Israel.
This is the 'Ephraimite Error.'"

Lew's response: My error comes from Scriptural references which clearly contrast the terms *"house of Israel"* and *"house of Yahudah"*, a division which developed after Dawid's conflict with Abshalom. The Yahudim are indeed among the Elect of YHWH, but there are *"other sheep who are not of this fold"*. Please don't put me into a box by thinking I believe that England and America are the primary remnants of the 10 lost tribes. Amos 9:9 tells us *"For look, I am commanding, and I shall sift the house of Israel among the Gentiles, as one sifts with a sieve, yet not a grain falls to the ground."* Ya'aqob 1:1 is addressed *"to the twelve tribes who are in the dispersion, Greetings!"* YirmeYahu 31 speaks of this "Ephraimite Error": *"For there shall be a day when the watchmen (Natsarim) cry on mount Ephraim, 'Arise, and let us go to Tsiyon, to YHWH our Elohim."* Then there are the end-time prophecies of the "two sticks" being made into one again, declared at Ezekiel 36 & 37, but if a person chooses to think these are Jews being regathered to Jews, then they are missing out on the revealed *secret of Elohim* which is being revealed just prior to the sounding of the 7th messenger (Rev. 10:7, Eph. 3:6). No harm done, but is this really an issue over which we have to become adversarial with one another? Shaul warned us to shun foolish controversies and genealogies - see 1 Tim. 1:4, and Titus 3:9. But, I like knowing that the 12 gates into the New Yerushaliyim will be named for each of the 12 tribes, because Yahushua is finding each one of us -- and others also who are engrafting. The 12 tribes (Israel) are the priests to the nations.

congregational leader: "He believes God has divorced Israel (p. 59) for her idolatry. Physical Israel no longer has a covenant with God unless they accept the New Covenant."

Lew's response: Odd that you would bring this up! If you turn to YirmeYahu 3, you will read about the treachery which the northern "house" (Israel) did after Dawid and Abshalom's conflict caused the division of the north and south. YHWH even says that the **house of Yahudah** did not return to Him from her backsliding even after witnessing what He had brought on the north (Israel was carried away!). He pleads with the house of Yahudah, telling her that her sister *(Israel of the north)* would not return to Him,

"But she did not return. And her treacherous sister Yahudah saw it. And I saw that for all the causes for which backsliding Yisrael had committed adultery (idolatry), I had put her away and given her a certificate of DIVORCE; yet her treacherous sister Yahudah did not fear; but went and committed whoring too." YirmeYahu 3:7,8.

congregational leader: "His use of "Paleo Hebrew" is outlandish and ridiculous, as there are many uncertainties about original character meaning and pronunciation. He believes that using "Paleo Hebrew" for God and Yeshua is the "only" correct way of representing them. He says the use of God is pagan and the use of Jesus/Yeshua is incorrect."

Lew's response: YHWH Elohim used palaeo-Hebrew to write the Torah in the stone tablets, so I stand on my choice of characters with Him. In fact, most of the prophets wrote in the archaic, primary Hebrew; it was only during the Babylonian Captivity that the Yahudim took the "Babylonian Hebrew" characters on -- Belshatstsar needed Daniel to read this "outlandish and ridiculous" script, because the Babylonians knew nothing of it. Mosheh, Abraham, Enoch, Dawid, Shlomoh -- these men could not read modern Hebrew; they used that "outlandish and ridiculous" palaeo-Hebrew script. The Great Scroll of Isaiah (YeshaYahu) is a copy of the original, and it is on display in the Shrine of the Book Museum in Yerushaliyim -- the Name is preserved in its original "outlandish and ridiculous" palaeo-Hebrew script, while the rest of the text is in modern Hebrew. The original is the Qodesh script, and must never be referred to in a profane or disrespectful manner. The letters (22) of both scripts have the same meanings and sounds (with some exceptions). The words mean the same things too. Alef is "ox", Beth is "house", and so on. Being a "living language", changes have occurred in the Hebrew tongue. But the script we call the palaeo-Hebrew was taught to Enoch by a messenger of YHWH (Book of Jubilees, source info). I have no axe to grind with the Aramaic whatsoever, but if we have to choose between them, I vote for the way my Father writes. We are babbling today, no doubt. Change is a form of corruption too. I can read both forms, both modern Babylonian/Aramaic as well as palaeo-Hebrew. I encourage everyone to draw closer to the original script, and for this I take a little heat once in a while.

congregational leader: His use of "Yahushua" is completely incorrect for representing Messiah.

Lew's response: Y'shua is fine with me, since it was written on Ya'aqob's ossuary in this way. But, it should not be dangerous to know that Y'shua is **short** for something, just as "Larry" is short for Lawrence. Yahshua is another fine rendering. Yeshua might NOT be alright, since it is attempting to modify the vowel for the sound of the Name, YAH. It seems to derive from "YESHU" (discussed more thoroughly in the fourth article in this book). We mustn't argue over words, but grow in understanding why we are using them. If a person wants to dig into it a little, the Greek texts at Acts 7 and Hebrews 4 will reveal the fact that "Joshua" and "Jesus" have the same underlying Greek letters, and so scholars have deduced that the two men actually have identical spellings in Hebrew. Greek is an intermediate language, and we know our Rabbi did not have a Greek name, nor did He ever hear "Jesus" on His eardrums. "Joshua" is spelled yod-hay-waw-shin-ayin. If you notice the spelling of "Yahudah", the first three letters also match this Name as well as the first three letters in YHWH, yod-hay-waw-hay. If the proper way to say yod-hay-waw-shin-ayin is not Yahushua, then I'm all ears to learn a better way.

congregational leader: "His use of Ha-Shatan is an incorrect use of the Hebrew language."

Lew's response: Shatan is word #7853, spelled shin-tet-nun, and means adversary or opponent. The prefix "ha" is simply an article equivalent to our word, "the". Is this something to get our hackles up over? Used as a pronoun, it is sometimes mistaken to be the same thing as a name; but in these cases it is merely a designation for a being who has, in fact, had his original name blotted out. The name this being had prior to its rebellion is easily researched; it is Azazel, meaning power of Elohim. Like us, this being has to go through time, so he doesn't exist in all time like YHWH does. If the word were spelled shin-tau-nun, it would mean "to urinate". They sound the same -- so that may be poetic justice. Now we're having fun!

congregational leader: "Throughout his book he has nothing good to say about anyone or anything, as he believes he is the only one who has the correct understanding."

Lew's response: I didn't realize that the book was not only depressing, but also taken to be a monument to conceit as well. I sincerely apologize if it was taken that way, but I recall stating that I merely gathered facts from many sources, and put them together -- not to judge people, but rather customs which had unsavory origins. Sure, most of the investigation is a major bummer, but trashing nonsense and doctrines against the Truth are difficult to present with a gleeful outcome. The wonderful news is, lots of people can investigate on their own to find out if what I've uncovered is true or not. Then they can gain the understanding and see how it feels to have eaten the "red pill" (analogy to Matrix). "With much wisdom comes much sorrow; the more knowledge, the more grief." Eccl. 1:18. I will pray for you, brother, to be granted wisdom in greater measure, and I hold no bitterness against you for your position. In the future, you will find that using Scripture to correct and rebuke error will work much better than personal feelings and popular opinions (just a friendly tip). "Preach the Word . . ." 2 Tim. 4:2.

congregational leader: "The entire book is incoherent and rambles endlessly back and forth between subjects and concepts. The book has no set order, theme, or consistent message."

Lew's response: The tapestry I chose to unravel is connected to many disciplines of knowledge, and what you said about the "rambling" back and forth is quite true -- but it is also true of the writings of brother Shaul. Reading **_FC_*** is not for entertainment. Many who have read it tell me they begin

_FC_: Fossilized Customs, another book by this author

to see more and more with their 2nd and 3rd reading. If it doesn't make sense to you, then read it again, and again, until the consistent message appears to you. Below, our brother rightly describes the contents of FC, calling them "abhorrent". I could not agree more. The deceptions that have been perpetrated upon all mankind are described more concisely by the messenger's words recorded by brother Yohanan:

"Babel the great is fallen, is fallen, and has become a dwelling place of demons, a haunt for every unclean spirit, and a haunt for every unclean and hated bird, because all the nations have drunk of the wine of the wrath of her whoring, and the sovereigns of the earth have committed whoring with her, and the merchants of the earth have become rich through the power of her riotous living." Rev. 18:2,3. If my worst sin is writing the book Fossilized Customs, exposing the deceptions and showing the Truth, then I am indeed relieved. The trouble is, I think I'm guilty of much worse -- I was doomed at one time without knowledge of Yahushua, and His love for me, and all His chosen ones.

As I reflect back to when I could not understand Scripture, I could have been guilty of having the same opinion of it, as you said of FC: "The entire book is incoherent and rambles endlessly back and forth between subjects and concepts. The book has no set order, theme, or consistent message".

congregational leader: Rick, as a result of these things, I feel it is inappropriate to be promoting a man with such deviate and unscriptural ideas. I think it would be in proper order to print a retraction in your next issue and warn people against this man and his book. I have had to deal with this book numerous times, as a number of people have been led astray by it's abhorent contents.

congregational leader: Feel free to use any of this in either direct or indirect quote.

Lew's response: I concur; circulate this in any way you like.

Next is a response I made to a brother who had received two letters regarding criticisms by the *Christian Research Institute*. Their criticisms and accusations against the "Sacred Name / Yahweh groups" are typical of most people who initially encounter Truth that may make them stretch beyond the box they are in. I guess those of us "outside the box" will seem like aliens to those who have closed them-selves off from more Truth.   Yahushua isn't a "Christian" . . . . .

Lew's response: I finally read the two letters they sent to you in response to the issues of the Name and so on. One of the letters acknowledged that the name "Jesus" is Greek. They didn't seem to hear what they were really saying by this obvious admission. To be technically accurate, "Jesus" isn't really Greek, but rather a Latinization based on the Greek. He also said that "Jesus" and "Yahshua" refer to the same Person. This is *quite true*, but one of the two **words** is a counterfeit for the "only Name" under Heaven given among men by which we must be saved (Acts 4:12).   He also was broad-stroking the definition of the word "name", yet when YHWH spoke of His Name, His intention was never for us to *substitute* it with other terms.   Also, Yahushua was quite specific when He referred to the Name, and His own.   He knew, obviously, that the nation of   Israel was not using the Name, and He stated He had "revealed" the Name to those the Father had given to Him (Yn. 17:6).   They didn't even know it until He used it, tradition had levied the penalty of death on anyone who would ever use it aloud.

The other letter made the "sacred Name groups" sound like some bizarre, cultish extremists. Actually, we're only obsessive and zealous for the Name, and the Torah.   This naturally seems alien to the religion "ABOUT" the Messiah, but not to we who seek the "Kingdom" (rulership) of YHWH.   We're not attempting to sneak over the wall, but we want to enter through the gate with a status of legitimacy.   We know the Name, the personal Name, of the One we serve.   Generic, vague references don't get the job done for us, because we have been given an awesome gift: a love for the only true Elohim, and His Son   -- the Name is keeping us in unity as His followers.   Everlasting life is linked directly to knowing YHWH (Yn. 17:3) and His Son.   Yahushua is the One who has authority over all flesh, and He gives everlasting life to all those whom YHWH has given to Him.   Yahushua prayed that we be guarded in the Name of YHWH, the Name YHWH gave to Yahushua (not that there are two Names, nor two "Beings").   The article started out discussing the lack of our belief in the "trinity", and never used any Scriptural criticisms for this, but instead brought up that there were some Messianic groups that did believe in a trinity, as if that was some sort of proof that we surely are wrong about this. I suppose the writer expected us to hear what he said about this, and respond with *"Oh, well, we didn't realize there were other Messianics who believe that YHWH is three Beings; we need to simply agree on that, and move on."*

Often we have a tendency to search out fine points on which to disagree, but I still accept everyone as a brother who has the belief in Yahushua. It is our **love for one another** that should be the unmistakable trait that the world should see, not all the arguing and divisions. They may not have the "walk" correct at all, but taking baby steps in the right direction means a whole lot in Yahushua's eyes. He is the light, and since He is in us, we are the light of the world for them to follow -- just like the shekinah pillar in the wilderness. We aren't policemen, but ambassadors. They will draw away from us if we keep using stun guns and bull prods on them; their struggle, and ours, is against authorities and principalities of wickedness of a spiritual nature. These principalities have sent many false doctrines/teachings out into the world, but overcomers (by Yahushua's power) will discern what is a lie, and what is Truth. They will admit that the false Sabbath they observe is not the same one that Yahushua observed when He was on Earth 2000 years ago, the Sabbath He declared He was **Master** of. Though they are blind, we are here to help guide them back to the path -- we are not here to ridicule or condemn them.

I probably won't find time to get in touch with the writers of the letters, but you are welcome to share my responses with them if you think it will help.

Response to a Second Critic of Fossilized Customs

Lew's opening remarks: The following is from an Email sent on 11-11-05 by a person who consulted her pastor for his opinion of certain information on this website concerning the NAME (www.fossilizedcustoms.com/transliteration.html). Her words are in italics, and her pastor's in quotes:

Emailer: *I don't know if you accept feedback by email, but I thought I would send it & if you can reply, that would be great. I read "Fossilized Customs" recently & wanted to see how the pastor (at the church I have been attending) would respond to* *some of the info, so I emailed him a link to your website. His initial response said that Jesus was the Greek transliteration of Joshua (or words to that effect). So I sent him the link to the article on the name of Jesus from your website & asked if he had seen that article. I copied the part of his reply that addresses it below:*

pastor: "I did go to their website and read the article on the name of Jesus. Let me tell you why it is false. The oldest fragments of the New Testament, some dating back to 125 AD long before there was a Roman Catholic Church and even longer before the Jesuits arrived, all use the Greek name Jesus as is found in the Greek New Testament sitting here on my desk. I would challenge these people to produce texts older than lets say P52 (Book of John, dated 125 AD) that don't use the name of Jesus. They can't because they don't exist. This is nothing more than a conspiracy theory similar to that of the DeVinci Code."

Emailer: *I did not expect to sway him to accept what I have read, so I am not necessarily disappointed with his response. I just reread the article & it still makes sense to me & I have no problem accepting what I have read so far. I started attending this church years ago because it was one of the few that taught from the bible verse-by-verse. The pastor started on the book of Hebrews last week. I thought that I would attend a few more times, maybe even through the teaching on the book of Hebrews. The more I consider it, the less inclined I am to return to that church or any other mainstream christianity group. I was raised catholic & was able to accept christianity after I finished high school. Now that I have read a couple of related books ("Nazarene Israel" & "Restoration") & had time to think & pray about it, accepting the re-newed covenant idea was not difficult at all. I almost feel like I need to be deprogrammed or detoxified or something from everything I have been taught up to this point. Thanks for your time.* [sender's name deleted]

Lew's response to Emailer: Thank you for your gentle boldness in sharing the Truth with your assembly's "shepherd" (pastor). This gentleman is fully aware that if he were to guide his sheep in the direction of the true Name, or promote obedience to the Covenant, he would lose about half of his assembly. The idea that the Greek letters IESOU and

IESOUS are the "final authority" for the real Name of our Messiah is promoted by all the seminaries and "Bible colleges", but all of these are off-shoots of Jesuit schools. The first universities and seminaries were Catholic Cathedral schools, and the protestants mimicked these. Remember also, the first protestants were all Catholics! This is why I can honestly say that the false name JESUS is a promotion of the Jesuits, who only want people to think about the Greek, and NEVER pay any attention to the original Hebrew. Magicians use one thing to their advantage: the skilled *art of misdirection* - the distraction in this instance is the Greek language. We are children of Light, and Truth; not misdirecton.

In the 4th century, a "church father" named Epiphanius wrote of a sect of "heretics" called NATSARIM that possessed a copy of the gospel of Matthew, as it was written in the original Hebrew. The Catholic-controlled scroll team (concerning the Dead Sea Scrolls) at Ecole Biblique has a copy of Matthew found in one of the caves in 1947, but they have not released it to be viewed by the world. These scrolls were retired to those caves for only one reason:
the NAME of the Creator was written on them.
This means that the copy of Matthew (Hebrew, "MattithYahu") also has the NAME written on it. But still we have the misguided impressions in seminary-trained men who think the GREEK is the final authority on this matter. The pastor's challenge was to produce texts OLDER than AD 125 **"that don't use the name Jesus".**
Sure, no problem; the *__Hebrew__ texts* like the book of "Joshua" (the same name), and the scroll of MattithYahu (Matthew) discovered in the DSS, but held captive by the RCC. We don't have to play the Greek game. There IS NO TEXT before 1530 CE that uses the spelling JESUS. The letter "J" didn't even exist until then. The "Geneva Bible" spelled the Messiah's Name IESUS. Does IESOU look or sound anything like JESUS? There is no letter "J" on this planet until around 1530. What does the name IESOU mean? What does the name JESUS mean? No one really knows. Yahushua means "Yah-is our-salvation", the same thing that "JOSHUA" (best "Yahushua") means. It's Hebrew; not Greek, Latin, English, or Japanese.

Since you will be studying Hebrews soon, note carefully

Hebrews chapter 4, and watch how they "spiritualize" the 4th Commandment (Sabbath). Origen's school at Alexandria, Egypt started some of our modern interpretations because everything drifted into "allegorical" meanings. Also, it's interesting that the GREEK text which underlies the English text uses the SAME LETTERS (IESOU) for both names, JESUS and JOSHUA (proof can be easily seen by looking at a Greek/English interlinear at Hebrews 4 and Acts 7). Scholars agree that since this is the case, both our Messiah and Mosheh's successor had THE SAME NAME. That name is spelled *yod-hay-waw-shin-ayin* in the Hebrew; anyone who searches this out can see it in the Hebrew texts. You might further challenge your pastor with my response here, to see how he might either accept or refute what I'm saying.

Pray for him, he may begin to see that our Rabbi Yahushua would not promote a fake Greek name, nor continue to teach His followers to ignore the true Sabbath (Hebrews 4), when He is the One who gave the Sabbath to mankind, and called it the "sign" of the eternal Covenant (see Ezekiel 20:12-20, Is. 56, Ex. 31:13-17). There is only one BODY, and that is ISRAEL, which former Gentiles (Eph. 2:8-13, Romans 11) must engraft into.

Stay positive about sharing the truth with everyone, but in small, bite-sized bits. The truth that you send into the world around you will bear fruit, like planting and watering. We're gardeners, and Yahushua is the Owner of the garden. People are the soil, waiting for the seed and watering we gardeners provide.

The thing we have to remember is that it takes time to see the fruit. We plant a seed of truth, but often want it to sprout ripe fruit right before our eyes. Just keep planting and watering, and Yahushua will bring forth the harvest. Your efforts are having a huge effect. When they talk about you behind your back it's proof that you are rustling their consciences. The truth will conflict with what they have come to believe, and it will have to be reconciled eventually. The truth never loses the battle against the principalities and powers of evil. The corruption we see in this world will be cleared-away, and what Yahushua plants in its place will be eternal and pleasing to Him.

May Yahushua use us all for His purposes, and produce a beautiful garden!

THE HEBREW CALENDAR   ISRAEL MEASURES TIME

A discussion on the 13-month controversy for some years, and the calculation for the 1st moon

This article concerns interpretation, not rebellion or condemnation. About every third year, we encounter some level of disagreement within Yahushua's body (Covenant people, Israel) over the necessary adjustment of the number of moons for that year -- and 2005 CE was one of those years. The "intercalating" (adding) of an extra month is sometimes needed to keep the seasons balanced with the months, so about 7 out of every 19 years needs to have 13 months. The last sitting Sanhedrin set up the standardized method for the calendar, so the only authority to overrule this would be the entire Body of Mashiach. The added moon (13th month) has to be done sometime, so why not just acknowledge it and do it in unity? Otherwise, we'll each be doing whatever is right in our OWN eyes, and observing the moedim (appointed High Sabbaths) at diverse times from one another. As you may know, there are divisions over this, concerning the sighting of the **barley** in Israel. A small quantity of some species of **uncultivated barley** is often noticeable, and some of this became almost ripe last month (written in spring "2005"), however the **harvest** of cultivated barley was certainly not ready. It was **still winter** when some proclaimed the discovery of the ripe wild barley. The **equinox** (Hebrew, a tequphah, or *te-kufah* #8622, *circuit*) is used in the calculation of the arrival of **springtime**; this is simply because we use a lunar/solar calendar (not strictly a lunar one as the Islamic world does). Permit me to explain this "year" thing, and how **Ex. 12:2** tells us that the arrival of the "first moon" of the year is in the SPRING/SUMMER cycle, not the fall/winter. Also, the barley doesn't determine when to watch for anything; we are simply told to bring a sheaf of the harvest (the cultivated crop planted) to the priest (SEE LEV. 23:10) -- and the whole crop is ready to be harvested, not just a patch of barley that is ripening that you had to go out and hunt down   (the barley taken to the priest is a cultivated crop of barley, not some wild growth blundered into -- it's <u>harvested</u>).   If each one of us privately interprets how and when to do things -- as it seems we are -- people are going to be very divided.   That's why we must search out the TRUTH of every matter carefully -- and it's not hard to do.Important to note: the BODY OF MASHIACH is to be our critic.   For example, the majority of Karaites are not currently believers in Yahushua.   So, let no one outside the body of Mashiach judge you in new moons, Sabbaths, food, drink, or a festival, BUT the body of Messiah. (Col. 2:16).   The Karaites may set the appointments differ-ently than some Natsarim, and we all work out the setting of the moed'im as well as we can possibly do it.   Some started out this year while it was still winter - seemingly ignoring the fact that the sun determines the days and YEARS for us, and unless Earth crosses the point of the spring equinox, it's still winter.   If Scripture says to look for the "**GREEN EARS**", and then to watch for the next new moon, my only question is, *WHERE does it say this?*   Seeing it spelled-out in Scripture will easily convince everyone of how to do things properly. I'm sure that none of us, on either side of this issue, are being willfully rebellious in the least.

ABIB - SPRING:
THE FIRST MOON OF THE YEAR (SPRING, EX. 12:2)

"Abib" means *ear*, or *grain*, but not a "green" ear.   The sun, moon, and stars are all used together for days, years, signs, and moedim (called "seasons", or appointments).   To-rah doesn't come out and actually say "equinox", but uses the word *TEKUFAH*; this is because the SUN (and Earth's rota-tion, tilt, & orbit around it) determines days and <u>years</u>.   It's not spring, **until** the equinox (tekufah) arrives.   If we begin *be-fore* the equinox, then our feast in the fall will begin at the end of summer, dragging everything *earlier* by a month.   While other places on Earth may have more pronounced seasonal variations producing 4 distinct seasons, the land of Israel has mainly 2: summer & winter.   Both begin with a marked in-crease in rain, giving us the "early" and "latter" rains (Dt. 11:14).   So, first we are to look for the arrival of the spring and its obvious "early rains", then watch for the ripening of the barley grains -- the WHOLE crop -- and when we harvest this crop, the "first fruits" of this harvest are to be taken before the High Priest, Who now is Yahushua, for Him to wave it before YHWH. So, "ABIB" would pertain to the ripe grain, harvested and taken from the planted crops to be waved by the High Priest. The barley plays no role presently, because there is no operating priesthood conducting any of the waving of the first fruits aspects of the instructions in Torah; we Natsarim know that Yahushua fulfilled this first fruits offering when He resurrected and presented Himself before YHWH. There has been a change in the priesthood - see Hebrews 8. Without an operational Temple with priests performing daily duties, and a high priest to physically satisfy the prescribed offerings, it becomes difficult to take a Nazirite vow, or bring barley, or do anything but seek out the lost sheep -- which is our duty now as priests according to the order of Melckizedek.

If anyone tells you they waved barley or took a Nazirite vow, ask them where they are hiding their time machine! So, the unbelieving Karaites don't agree with us on every point. Ultimately, it's not BARLEY, but it's YAHUSHUA they should have been watching for. The barley was a metaphor or allegory which pointed to Yahushua. Now, when we see the full barley crop ready to be harvested, we can better appreciate what Torah was pointing at. Yahushua is the first harvest, and we His qodeshim (saints) are part of a group of the first fruits; the larger wheat harvest in the fall are those who respond to our planting and watering work. See? It's all about "shadows" of meaning -- we need to be more concerned about the meaning behind the actual grains growing in the ground. Many Messianics have been taught that we are to watch for "green ears", then watch for the next new moon; but this is not what is to be done according to Scripture. It's a delusion intended to deceive, and has succeeded marvelously.

As Rob Miller explained it so well, *"Since the discrepancy between the solar and lunar years amounts to 207 days every 19 years, the "leap month" of Adar Sheni is added to the third, sixth, eight, eleventh, fourteenth, seventeenth and nineteenth year of every nineteen year period, that is, seven times in a 19-year lunar cycle."* In other words, 7 years out of every 19 years **must** have 13 months -- so the last sitting Sanhedrin ordained that a month is to be added, or "intercalated", making those years have an ADAR I and an ADAR II. This past year was one of these (2005 CE), and some resist it because they saw a few grains of barley get ripened. The WHOLE barley harvest must be ready to harvest, and ready to reap: *"When you come into the land which I give you, and shall reap its harvest, then you shall bring a sheaf of the first-fruits of your harvest to the priest."* Lev. 23:10. The barley plays an important part, but it still is the "finger" pointing to Yahushua, our true "first-fruit offering", Who offered Himself to the Father. To keep looking at the finger (barley) is a very foolish thing to do -- it signifies the Mashiach, Who "waved" (was dead, then came back to life) before Father YHWH.

PESACH, Passover: (ref. Lev. 23, Dt. 16)

The evening of the 14th of Abib (Nisan), as we understand it, is at the beginning of the 14th, rather than in the end of the 14th (*"there was <u>evening</u>, and there was <u>morning</u> . . ."*).

The western mind thinks "evening" is at the END of each day, but Scripturally the "evening" marks the **beginning** of each day.   Yahushua stated He desired to eat the Passover meal *before* He suffered; yet even in those days there were differences among the Yahudim regarding the arrival of the "evening" of the 14th of Abib.   While He was hanging on the tree, the Yahudim pleaded for Pilate to have His body taken down, BEFORE the arrival of the High Sabbath Day -- the 15th of that moon.   It states they did not wish to enter the building because they did not wish to defile themselves, that they might "eat the Passover".   At the same time, the text admits that the "High Sabbath" (the 15th, beginning Unleavened Bread) was approaching that sunset.   They **combined** the Passover observance with the first day of Unleavened Bread, as we see they continue to do today.   Yahushua must have eaten the Passover with His talmidim at the **beginning** of the 14th day, which started at sunset, and later the same night He was arrested in the garden.   Using the Roman date to help illustrate, we will observe the death of Yahushua (Pesach, Passover) at sunset on April 22, just as the weekly Shabbat arrives.   The following sunset, as the weekly Shabbat ends, another "evening" heralds the arrival of a new day, the High Shabbat of the 1st day of Unleavened Bread.   So, a weekly Shabbat will be immediately followed by the first High Shabbat of the new year.   This High Sabbath is the "full moon" of YHWH's first month, and is exactly the 15th of the moon. If you begin your "count" from the *sighting* of the sliver moon at sunset to begin the first day of the moon, instead of sighting the sliver just before the *sunrise* and waiting a day, your High Sabbath (feast) will more than likely be one day later, so the moon will not be exactly "full" when you count to the 15th, and observe your first day of Matsah. The orthodox use the conjunction (dark moon), not the sliver sighting. Many believe *two witnesses* must go out and "see" the new moon, and report it to the elders. Sorry, there's no Scripture on that, only Talmudic sources (human tradition). Always check to see if the moon is FULL on your feast, since it states at Ps. 81:3: *"Blow the ram's horn at the time of the new moon, at the full moon, on our festival day."* So, the evidence is strongly leaning toward the 15th being the full moon, testing whether your starting point is correct. It *doesn't* say "the day *after* the full moon, on our festival day", so the moon can definitely clue us into whether we're on time. This is being mentioned in kindness, not to be severe or judgmental at all. All we can do is our best, and where we all fall short of perfection, Yahushua can take care of -- He knows we can be "wrong", but not in rebellion. We still love all those who observe with a different understanding — the moed'im are "shadows" . . . our family of believers, — and the love between us all — is our biggest test of faithfulness. That love for one another is the how the world will know we are Yahushua's talmidim. Voy Wilks of the Assembly of Yahweh (Cisco, TX) has this to say about the equinox topic:

Equinox - A TEKUFAH

The equinox occurs because of the (apparent) action of the sun. The earth, which is tilted 23.5 degrees, circles the sun, creating our seasons (spring, summer, fall and winter). The equinox occurs when the sun "crosses" the equator. The Hebrew word is tekufah, and refers to the solstices as well as to the equinoxes.

Tekufot (plural) means "seasons;" literally, "circuit, to go round." The four seasons in the year are called tekufot. More accurately, tekufot is the beginning of the four seasons. ... tekufah stands for the true, not the mean, equinox.

The tekufah (singular) **of Nisan** denotes the sun at the vernal equinox.

The next tekufah denotes the summer solstice.
The third tekufah denotes the fall equinox.
The fourth tekufah denotes the winter solstice.

Tekufah appears in the Scriptures four times, and relates to the calendar at least three times.
"And it came to pass at the end [tekufah] of the year, that the Syrians came up against him: .." (2Chr. 24:23).

This refers to the end and, therefore, the **beginning** of another year, demarcated by the spring equinox and the new moon.
"And you shall observe the feast of weeks, even the firstfruits of wheat harvest, and the feast of ingathering at the years end [tekufah]" (Ex. 34:22).
This refers to the fall equinox, the end of the summer growing season.

"In them [the heavens] he has set a tent for the sun, which comes forth like a bridegroom leaving his chamber, and like a strong man runs it's course with joy. It's rising is from the end of the heavens and it's circuit [tekufah] *to the end of them, and there is nothing hid from it's heat."* (Ps. 19:4,5 RSV)

This speaks of the sun's daily course, or it's yearly circuit through the equinoxes and the solstices, or both.
"And it came to pass, when the time was come [tekufah] *about, that Hannah concieved, and bore a son; ..."* (1Sam. 1:20) This may indirectly allude to the calendar year. In any case, the above Scriptures indicate that the saints of old understood the equinox and it's place in the calendar."
(end of Voy Wilks quote)

QUESTIONS - AND STATEMENT OF FAITH
A friendly peek at some interesting questions, and Lew's short answers.

Q: My name is (name withheld) and I'm 30 yrs old. My question is, one of the bumper stickers that was sent reads "Do wet rocks give birth?" Please explain that to me. I don't know what it means (so when I'm asked I can have a response). You might be wondering "why did he buy it, if he doesn't understand it?" Well actually I didn't buy that one. The one I purchased was the one that reads "If you believe there's no creator you better be right." Anyway either one will get the job done.

[Lew's short answer]   Oops - we sent the wrong sticker. This phrase, "Do Wet Rocks Give Birth?", was thought-up by Norman Willis, and I admit it is quite a stumper at first, but thought-provoking.   What I think Norman is trying to say is that life involves more design than evolutionists' ideas give it credit for having -- and you can't fix this by adding time to the situation.   In fact, evolutionists believe that the chemicals and minerals in rocks were dissolved by rain, then these arranged themselves to form long chains of amino acids, proteins, and eventually DNA and chromosomes.   All they have to do is ignore the 2nd law of thermodynamics, and assume that a fully-functioning eyeball will eventually emerge from the ooze, because that's what the matter in the universe really wants to be -- it just needs time to get organized.   Their efforts to figure out a way to explain life without a designer is the pinnacle of hypocrisy, which seems to know no bounds.   Denial isn't just a river in Egypt.   Even if something were to "spontaneously" generate, it would have to find the perfect mate with which to propagate itself.   Sexual reproduction is perhaps the biggest problem of all for evolutionists.

Q: I also have another question. I read the book Fossilized Customs, and in it you talk about the movie the Matrix. I saw that movie, and it's one of my favorites. As believers, is it wrong to do "worldly things" like go to the movies, learn Karate, go skiing etc...

[Lew's short answer]   The "rules of men" have added a great deal to the religions, and this has been going on since the beginning.   The Torah is about love - (of YHWH and the life of people and all the living things He's created).   Respect for life is one goal of religion hopefully.   When we damage another's reputation we have crossed the line.   We can drink wine, beer, and even whiskey -- in moderation.   We can dance.   We can live in this world, with sin all around us, yet not be of the world.   If we never drink anything but orange juice and water, never dance, never turn to the left, never learn to drive, never have sex, never play harmonica, or never whatever, we are not going to be guilty of doing anything wrong -- we've simply decided to avoid several things.   This doesn't change our hearts however.   Some will not allow the

female arm to be seen unclothed above the elbow. Smiling was considered a sign of insanity for most of human history -- that's why all the busts and paintings have such grim expressions, and also why the painting called the "Mona Lisa" caused such a big stir.

We can do anything that the Torah permits us to do. What the Torah forbids, we do not do. When we add extra prohibitions, and feel we are becoming more "pious", the only one being deceived is ourselves -- but I doubt we're "missing-out" on any great amount of fun either. If we completely avoid the sinner, cutting ourselves off from all contact with those we "judge" to be immoral, we are useless to help them. If they don't wish to be concerned with growing to become better, then we should avoid them. We are salt, which is spread sparingly, and very preciously. Salt can be uncomfortable at times too, to its surroundings -- and be uncomfortable because of its surroundings (it can melt or dissolve away). The goal of the prohibitions against certain activities was simply to keep believers away from the influences of Pagans and fleshly people who might corrupt the "good" people. We know there are not any "good" people, since all of us are sinners, and fall short. We become stronger through trials, by encouraging one another; so having another believing friend or spouse helps us stand against errors. This is likely why Yahushua sent them in pairs, to be of help to one another. Marriages are also like this, and back-to-back, we are stronger and very likely to overcome. Not many of us are sent into the trenches of the front lines of spiritual warfare, as Yahushua was criticized for being around the "sinners" of His time. But our best work is found at the cutting edge of the frontier between the people of the world living in darkness, and the struggling children of light who are sent to show them back to the path of life. We are only preserved by the power of Yahushua, Who is doing His marvelous work in us -- but we are sometimes severely wounded by our friends, who are critical because they don't understand. (Father, forgive them, for they know not what they do). We, like Stephen (Acts 7), are sometimes attacked by the religious community of believers we are part of.

Concerning "evolution" and a major reason for its rise: NEGLECTING TO OBSERVE THE SABBATH DAY

(remembering to rest, stop working)

A belief in "evolution" is a natural response in people who have "forgotten" about their Creator. The 4th Commandment to YHWH's wife/bride (Israel, not just "Jews") tells us to "remember" the Sabbath, BECAUSE YHWH created the heavens and Earth in six days and rested the 7th (also see Heb. 4). The answer is in Genesis 1, all through Acts, Hebrews, Isaiah 56, Ez. 20, and another 100 places on this topic. The 7th Day of each week is established as a COMMEMORATION OF CREATION, honoring the One Who is the true Creator. We are the servants of the one whom we OBEY; if we are deceived by a deceiver, given an excuse to change the Commandment, then we don't know we've been deceived until someone comes along and tells us. Now, you've been told. The wicked have "no rest", or Sabbath. The Sabbath Day is the "sign" of the Everlasting Covenant. This sign brings persecution, because: The adversary changed the Sabbath Day to the Romans' "Day of the Sun" in 321 CE. (by the authority of the first "pope" of Catholicism, Constantine I)

In contrast, the Natsarim follow the Messiah of Israel, and love Him enough to obey His Commands, which are not grievous or difficult.

Natsarim (from NATSAR, #5341; branch, guard, watch, observe, watcher).Why are we called that? Because we are the watchmen; we are the ones who call out at midnight, Matt. 25:1-13, Mark 13:34-37. Acts 24:5 calls our sect "the Natsarim", and Shaul was accused of being a "ringleader". Ephraim: the appointed watchmen—YirmeYahu 31:6, Hos. 9:8.We are the alert ones; and we are announcing the end of the times of the Goyim. Prepare to meet the Bridegroom; Blessed is the One Who comes in the Name of YHWH, REPENT FOR THE REIGN OF YHWH DRAWS NEAR.

As a prelude to what follows, I'd like to say these few words:

As we each increase in our knowledge in the true faith, we may find that many things we believe to be true may have no bearing on our salvation, but we find ourselves haggling over them quite often. Confrontations over silly issues often become heated debates. We're always fine-tuning ourselves, so we need to give each other a little room to do that. By approaching the Scriptures with a previous belief system, many think they find proof of what they believe in Scripture (This is faulty, and called "*eisegesis*"). But, we should let the Scriptures teach us what to believe (exegesis), not carry a belief into our "reading" of them. There are many teachings on many things floating about, and most are not salvational. For example, although I believe the Great Flood (of Noach's day) was global in scope, many believers are convinced it was 400 miles long and 100 miles wide, near the Black Sea. So, I don't reject a believer over thinking differently on this, but I wonder how they can arrive at their conclusions in the face of Scriptural texts. I also resort to simple logic, and by reasoning together sometimes our differences can be resolved. Why would Noach spend 100 years building an ark, when all he really needed to do was migrate for 3 weeks?

Usually, I view setting up doctrinal statements as a possible avenue of division among us, but I'm glad to answer direct questions. Please understand that my positions on certain matters may only be "leaning" in a particular direction, and it certainly doesn't isolate my thinking or close off my interest in what others lean toward, may choose to believe, or interpret. I respect everyone's opinions, and I consider their views valuable as long as the doctrines are not working against our obedience to the teachings of YHWH.

The questions below will provoke some thought, and they will be followed by a Statement of Faith. In some respects, fixed statements of doctrine can serve to divide the Body of Mashiach, but if they are not traditions of men brought over into our faith, but come solely from Scripture, then it does no harm to make a list of those things which help frame our faith.

QUESTIONS I'VE BEEN ASKED

Q: The Bible - Do you believe that English speaking people have the Holy infallible Word of God?

Answer: Barring lawless footnotes and certain errors in translation, our Scriptures contain, in general, the English equivalent to the ideas expressed in the original inspired Hebrew. I believe the original Hebrew is the infallible source. Concerning the Greek texts, the Catholic copyists seem to have altered the Messianic writings to such an extent that no two sentences in the Greek match perfectly among the many copies, but in general I believe that YHWH would not allow us to be overly deceived. He does have ha shatan on a leash, so errors can be overcome. We can listen to Scripture with a lawless ear, and come away believing we don't have to obey; or we can listen with an ear willing to learn and obey. This is what Yahushua meant by our eye being "filled with light", or "filled with darkness" -- it's all a matter of how our Spiritual world-view is slanted.

Q: What position do you take regarding the doctrine of the trinity?

Answer: Our human tradition of the teaching about the "triune nature" of YHWH doesn't originate from Scripture. Reading only Scripture, it would be highly unlikely for anyone to develop a "trinitarian" concept, they would need to be taught this first, then bring it with them to the study. The "Trinity" entered the belief through what is called The Apostles' Creed, formulated as an integral part of the rite of baptism (This "rite" is not the same act as we find in Scripture). A clearly divided and separate confession of Father, Son, and Holy Ghost, corresponding to the Divine Persons invoked in the formula of baptism was imposed by Catholicism, and this dogma has persisted strongly to the present. This Creed developed from a primitive teaching (c. 390), and is referred to in a letter addressed to Siricius by the Council of Milan (Migne, P.L., XVI, 1213), which supplies the earliest known instance of the combination Symbolum Apostolorum ("Creed of the Apostles"). Certainly any idea that it actually originated with the 12 Apostles is a myth. The actual inception of the doctrine of the Trinity seems to be best explained as coming from the Nicene Creed, formulated under the Emperor Constantine in 325 AD. "Non-Catholic" Christians are still 95% the same as Catholics, but they don't realize it. Pagan trinities abound, and it was Constantine I who brought this doctrine into the Messianic faith at the Council of Nicea in 325 CE. I don't judge the issue as salvational, but it served the purposes of early people in authority to bring Pagans into an understanding of the teachings of the followers of Yahushua, but explained by means of Pagan models. In Christianity, most every observance came from Paganism, but these observances were used to illustrate a truth or teaching found in Scripture. This is like using the format of WITCHCRAFT to explain the salvation plan of YHWH. Rather than simply repenting of the behavior and obeying how Scripture shows us to live, our forebears adopted the processes and calendar of Paganism instead. YHWH is Spirit, and He has manifested Himself to us in many ways over time. The last time He spoke to us through His Son. We who have been convicted of our sins and repented, He has come into us and written His Torah (teachings) on our hearts and minds -- thus circumcising our hearts in the New Covenant.

It would be accurate to say that I'm not a Trinitarian, but I respect those who are as long as they hold to the teaching of YHWH by obeying the Commandments, and the testimony of Yahushua. Yahushua's Command for us to love one another is not contingent upon whether a person is dividing YHWH into 3 parts or not. He judges our hearts, and we are all a "work in progress". No one has it all perfectly figured out, except Him. When we reject someone, we have judged them, and this rejection will enter into how we will be judged when our time comes. Simply put, I'm not a trinitarian -- but I love people who are.

Q: Do you believe in the physical resurrection of Yahshua?

Answer: Yes, and in this is our only hope. If Yahushua is not raised, then our faith is in vain, and we are to be pitied more than all men. Yahushua's resurrection was apparent to Peter and Yahuchanon, because they could see the wrappings that had been glued in place around His body were still undisturbed -- but the body was gone and the wrappings were still undisturbed! He passed through the wrappings, and the hillside that imprisoned Him. I have nothing to do with the celebration of "Easter Sun-day", although I identify each believers' immersion with Yahushua' death, burial, and resurrection. His resurrection doesn't need to be framed in a Pagan background for anyone to understand it.

Q: Do you believe in the doctrine of a rapture of the saints? If so, do you believe this will happen before, during or after the tribulation period?

Answer: If we are alive at Yahushua's return, I believe we will be gathered in the air first to meet Yahushua, preceded by the dead in Yahushua, and this occurrence will be after the tribulation. This will be when our flesh will change into incorruption in the wink of an eye. The tribulation will be very evident to everyone alive, and the "elect" of YHWH will be present during the entire duration, regardless of what books and movies tell us about it. The people "DEAD" who will be raised incorruptable at Yahushua's coming must not be "in heaven", since they will awaken when He calls them out of their graves. The chosen (elect) will be alive, and changed in the twinkling of an eye, not raptured away in advance of the great trib; their "rapture" will be when they are clothed with immortality. The days will be shortened (the length of the great trib) for the sake of the chosen.

Here's what Scripture says:

"For then there will be great tribulation, such as has not been since the beginning of the world until this time; no, nor ever shall be. And unless those days were shortened, no flesh would be saved; BUT FOR THE ELECT'S SAKE, those days will be shortened." (Mt. 24:21,22)

IF THE ELECT ARE NOT STILL ON THE EARTH, THEN THE DAYS WOULD NOT NEED TO BE SHORTENED. So, we can easily see that the "ELECT" (Israel of YHWH -- all 12 tribes) will be on Earth to the bitter end, not whisked up in the air like the books and movies say it will happen. The elect will be the reason that this horrible tribulation will be SHORTENED. The parable of the wheat and tares (weeds) is also an illustration of the timing of the harvesting of the Earth. The harvest of the Earth is one of the "mysteries" of the Kingdom of YHWH (Mt. 13:11). Mattit Yahu 13 is full of the examples of how it will be. At Mt. 13:24-30, in the parable of the wheat and tares, the workers asked:

"Do you want us, then, to go and gather them (the weeds) up?" But He said 'No; lest while you are gathering up the tares, you may root up the wheat with them. Allow both to grow together UNTIL THE HARVEST; and in the time of the harvest I will say to the reapers, 'FIRST, GATHER UP THE TARES and bind them in bundles to burn them up; but gather the wheat into my barn.'" (See also Mt. 3:12)

The "rapture cult" believes the elect will be spared the tribulation because they infer the wrong order of things from

Paul's writings, and completely ignore the parables because they are spiritually discerned "mysteries".

Q: Do you believe in a literal hell, as being an eternal place of punishment for the wicked and unbelieving?

Answer: HELL -- This word is from the Old English word "hell", meaning "hole". It referred to a place below ground, and became the popular word used by translators to convey the concept of Gahanna in Greek, from the Hebrew "SHEOL", which is either a literal grave, or used to refer to the state of the dead. The fiery destruction of the unrighteous in Scripture seems to be having themselves tossed into what is called "YAM ESH", meaning "lake of fire". This is also called "the SECOND death". The *first death* is required of all flesh, but the SECOND death seems to be the permanent eradication of the spirit being of each unrighteous creature. A "death" implies and end to something.

The "breath of life" has been said to apply to only the physical life (nephesh) by some, but I tend to go one step beyond this idea, and take it to include the "living soul" also (some say this is a concept from Paganism). Our spirit or nephesh comes from YHWH, Who is Spirit, and "it" returns to Him also. It may be more than oxygen's chemical reaction with our physical composition. Scripture speaks of our "spirit" as well. The state of the unrighteous may end up simply as recycled spirit energy at their second "death". Now, I am not dogmatically opposed to the possibility that there may also be "eternal punishment", existence apart and without YHWH, but if there is, then this would *ALSO* be "eternal life"; this is why I only tend to lean toward the idea that the unrighteous may not be around to suffer. They may, but this presents a logical conflict -- eternal life is eternal. If a creature is to be punished for *all eternity*, it would also seem to be necessary to have *eternal life* (a conscious existence) to sustain them for the torture. Another thing about the idea of eternal punishment is, it seems outside of YHWH's goals and character. He would not have one of us torture another creature, and being Creator, and the embodiment of love, He probably would simply destroy the unrighteous. The texts that seem to say "eternal burning" and "smoke that rises forever" could be idioms. "Hell" has been used to put fear into men's hearts, and if this gets some peoples' attention, it serves well enough. I'm mostly concerned for the unrepentant because of the loss of eternal life they will suffer. They just don't realize the enormity of such a loss.

Q: How can a person go to heaven?   Is keeping Yahweh's commands required for salvation?

Answer: These two questions are very much related. The entire Brit Chadasha (New Covenant) discusses the Kingdom of Heaven (or more accurately, the Kingdom of YHWH). The lawless, murderers, liars, idolaters, perverts, and general YHWH-haters will not enter the Kingdom, called the world-to-come by many. The pure in heart (those without hate for YHWH or His Creation) provide ample proof of their inner nature by their thoughts and actions. Yahushua was asked how a person could inherit the Kingdom of YHWH, and His answer was "Keep (observe, practice) the Commandments". This is impossible for those in the "mind of the flesh", meaning they serve their flesh. Those who walk "in the mind of the Spirit" do that which is after the Spirit, and their fruits are love, joy, peace, patience, kindness, goodness, gentleness, faithfulness, and self-control. The Commandments are spiritual, and the mind of the flesh cannot obey without being led by the Spirit, so if we don't have the Spirit of Mashiach, we are not His, and will not inherit the world-to-come.

Q: What commands are we to keep?

Answer: This is the question which Yahushua answered the young man who asked Him how to inherit the Kingdom of YHWH. Yahushua began to enumerate the Torah Covenant, at Exodus 20. For a long and blessed life, one should also pay attention to the laws at Lev. 11, 19, 23, and observe the annual moedim (appointments) at Deut. 16.   Yesha Yahu (Isaiah) 56 closely ties in the observance of His **Sabbaths** with salvation (verse 6).   The Redemption plan of His bride/wife (Israel) is fore-shadowed in the seven annual High Sabbaths.

Q: How are we to keep the Sabbath?

Answer: A Shakespearian way of asking this might be,
        *"To **rest**, or not to **rest**; that is the question."*

The Sabbath is about one thing: identification with the Creator because He rested during the first week of Creation. How is it observed? Every 7th day, Israel of YHWH is to REST from work. Do that, and you have satisfied the requirement. Israel had to be trained in how to do this also, and for 40 years YHWH used the manna (not the moon) to show them. "Let no man go out of his place on the Sabbath" (Ex. 16:29) is a favorite example I like to use, so if we stay in our vicinity and rest, we have accomplished what is implied by the Commandment. If you are unconscious for the entire duration of the 7th day, you have done no wrong. Doing relaxing things is certainly O.K. too. The Sabbath was given to us, we weren't given to it. It's YHWH's Sabbath, and one important aspect of it is that it is a commemoration of Creation, how we imitate YHWH by resting as He rested (Heb. 4).

The logical result or consequence of not remembering the Sabbath is: belief in evolution. At the setting of the Sun on the 6th day, beginning at evening (or twilight), my family gathers around the dining table to break bread, drink of the fruit of the vine, and I place the Name on my children (Aharonic example, Num. 6:22-27). This practice simply serves to "separate" the profane days of the week from the qodesh day, although it's not required; but you can develop family "tradition" that helps mark the time clearly in the minds of the growing children. We relax and play together as a family unit mostly, enjoying Creation. We work during the week for 6 days, and rest and relax on the 7th. Acts 20 shows that the Natsarim gathered **after** the Sabbath in someone's house, and Paul spoke until midnight (overly long because he planned to leave the next morning). The word "shabua" is Hebrew for week. At the end of the Shabbat, it was dark and considered to be "the first of the week". So, it was the beginning of the evening of the 1st day of the week when they actually assembled in that community. If there were a place nearby my home, and people were gathering there to study, I'd certainly go for a couple of hours each Sabbath. 1 Cor. 14:26 states that when we assemble, EACH ONE has a teaching, a prophecy, a tongue (language), and so not just one person dominates the group -- Yahushua speaks through each of us to His body.

Q: What is your religious background? Were you raised up in a specific church or denomination?

Answer: My parents raised me and my 4 brothers in their system of beliefs, which was (and still is to them) Roman Catholicism. I was trained throughout elementary school by nuns, and in high school by Jesuits. From the age of 18 to 22, I served in the U.S. Air Force. The next 7 years were spent earning a Bachelors degree at the University of Louisville Business school. I continued to study the sciences every spare moment, but only found human conjectures. The Roman Catholicism I had been raised with had faded, and I was no longer "drunk" by the programming. I now hold that system to be filled with the grossest idolatry imaginable, and most likely is the seat of the Anti-messiah. I was taught to kneel and talk to a cracker/cookie, which the priest-craft teaches everyone to believe is the living body of "Jesus" because the "priest" uttered the words "HOC EST CORPUS MEUM" over the cookie. When I had to time to investigate the history of Catholicism and its practices, it led to my study of various sciences -- since I just wanted the Truth. Later, I turned to the Scriptures for my answers, and only there could I find them. Those who are Christians but not Catholics may have a "tag" or denominational name for their sect/group. They are a few small steps out of Babylon, because they are not Catholic in their method of worship; but, they are still 95% like a Catholic, but don't know it. They still have Sun-day, Easter, Christmas, and lawlessness they feel is justified because in their own words they may claim they don't have to "obey" certain Commands because "we're not Jewish". The truth is, Israel is 12 tribes, and the Jews (Yahudim) are only one of them; the 12 gates of the New Jerusalem are named for these 12 tribes, and there's *not a single gate* that is for Catholics or Christians. You MUST engraft into ISRAEL, to partake of the Covenant and the promises (Rom. 11). Being "chosen" before the foundation of the world, the House of Israel (10 lost tribes) were sifted / dispersed into the nations (Amos 9:9), but they will be regathered and joined to the House of Yahudah in the END TIMES (see Ezek. 36 & 37) -- they were 2 sticks, but will be made into ONE STICK in YHWH's hand. Come out of her, my people! Come back to YHWH's House, and obey the Covenant - the bread you hunger for. Catholicism? All it offers is the "sacraments", a deceptive alternative to receiving the Truth, dispensed through a man-made priest craft. Being a Christian means you've left 5% of this system, and you need to come all the way out. Just as Yahuah once called Israel out of Egypt, He is now calling to His people again, *"Come out of her My people!"*

Q: If you previously were attending a different church denomination, was there a specific event that lead to your leaving the denomination you were previously involved in?

Answer: Being 18 years of age, I entered the U.S. Air Force. This was the first break in my life from being enslaved to the weekly Paganism / witchcraft I was involved in. After having time to reason through the incredible farce I had been involved in, I carefully evaluated whatever I decided to be Truth from then on. *Personal research* revealed more and more errors to me that were found in the religious traditions practiced by most denominations, so I approached the subject of religion from the standpoint of *Yahushua's own religion*. Going solely by what Scripture tells us, there was quite a lot of excess baggage that I could put down -- it was a load that I was glad to be relieved of carrying. Being in any "denomination" lays a *different* foundation than that which was laid, so denominations are Scripturally illegal - our only foundation is Yahushua. His "religion" is not Christianity, but rather He is the High Priest of YHWH, serving as a Priest forever, according to the order of Melkizedek. Yahushua is the Mashiach of Yisrael, into which Gentiles must "engraft", and not longer will they remain Gentiles (Eph. 2:8-13).

Q: Do you believe that all Anglo Saxons are part of the lost tribes of Israel?

Answer: The more proper Scriptural term is "House of Israel", which was sifted into the Gentiles over 2700 years ago by the Assyrians. See Amos 9:9, Ezek. 36 & 37, and take special notice of YirmeYahu (Jer.) chapter 3:6-25, and the distinction between what YHWH calls "sisters", by the terms "Israel" and "Yahudah". In general, I feel that the "lost 10 tribes" of the House of Israel are in the 100's of millions now, and are not primarily in one place, nor one "race". Abraham's name means "father of nations", and he is literally so through the 12 tribes of Israel. After the disruption between King

David and his son Absalom, there was a split between the "north" (the House of Israel, 10 tribes in Samaria), and the "south" (the House of Yahudah). This is important to comprehend if you wish to see the whole picture more clearly. Yahushua tried to calm the hatred between the House of Yahudah and those remnants living in the "north", called "Samaritans", because they are Israel also. He even declared that He was only sent to the lost sheep (lost tribes) of the House of Israel. They are the "prodigal son". It is probably true that many are now among the Anglo-Saxons; but I feel certain that the Ethiopians and many other black and Oriental peoples are also of the lost 10 tribes. Yahushua, in us, is still seeking these "lost sheep" today. The founding fathers of the USA believed that the native Americans were of the lost tribes of Israel. The Ethiopian eunuch was a Cushite (descendant of Cush, a black gentleman, Acts 8:26-40) and Philip helped him understand Yesha Yahu 53. I'm not one of those "White is Israel" people at all. Most probably, a GREAT many Hispanics are a mixture of all 12 tribes, since ancient Spain was known as Tarshish, and later "Safarad", seen today in the word "Sfard". It was Israel (all 12 tribes) who settled the ancient land of what is now Spain, even before Solomon's time. The book of Yonah discusses Tarshish, the region settled by Israelites in what is now southern Spain. The time of "Ya'aqob's trouble" may partly involve trying to sift through the catastrophe of being dispersed among the Gentiles, sown by YHWH (Amos 9:9). In the end, Israel is he or she who obeys the Covenant - get over your genealogy, and accept your brothers and sisters without vexation.

It has been hypothesized that the "coat of many colors" worn by Yosef (the technicolor dreamcoat) has been echoed down through the descendants of Ephraim, and found itself in the colorful "government of Tartan" we see in the plaids of Scot Land. The Angles are all of the same same stock, so the Scottish, Irish, and English may have among them much Ephraimite blood. In the Tartan system, one color means you're low-born, 2 means your family line is more important, and if your family colors are 3 or more, it's a really big deal. The one who wears the most colors is the ruler of all, and this reflects back to Yosef -- quite possibly. In my estimation, any who re-program their lives to the Torah are Israelites, and they are called by YHWH to be children engrafted -- no branches are to look askew at the others! YermeYahu 31 tells us of the "hills of Ephraim" (a term referring to the descendants of Yosef, who are not "Jews"), and from these "watchmen" (Hebrew NATSARIM) will arise when YHWH rebuilds the maiden of Israel, also called Ephraim. Read all of YermeYahu (Jer.) 31. YHWH is bringing forth the remnant before our eyes.

Instead of worrying about bloodlines, I am more concerned with who is awakening to the Truth, and if they are thirsty to learn, then YHWH is calling them. They become chosen when they are immersed into the Name of Yahushua, and this is their circumcision into the faith of Abraham, Yitzhak, and Ya'akob. Then, I know beyond all doubt they are included in the household of Israel. Read about "interracial marriage" below for some "culture shock" many are not prepared to accept.

Q: Many people past and present claim to be saved by believing in Jesus Christand calling on his name. Because these people have not used the Hebrew name
Yahushua do you believe that Yahweh will accept them? What will be their fate?

Answer: This is a very good question! We will be judged mostly by the measure we use to judge, so Yahushua wisely instructed us to "judge not". He indicated that those in ignorance would receive few blows, but those who knew and did not act on their knowledge would receive many blows. At this point in time, my best guess about why most people are taught to believe that the Messiah's Name is "Jesus" is because it has been aggressively promoted by the "Jesuits", a Catholic sect of priests called "the *Society of Jesus*". Their name says it all. The Jesuit-General is also referred to as the "Black Pope". They explain the Messiah's name in English by-way-of Greek. They also use Latin. The Hebrew is avoided, and by the time the listener is exposed to their Greco-Latinisms, they are probably sorry they ever brought it up. Some of us simply won't give up, and keep on pressing for more Truth. As I said, we are all a "work in progress", and it is never my intention to offend or injure the faith of a new believer by personal criticisms on their condition at a given snapshot in time. As we grow in understanding, we find

Scriptural reasons to abandon practices which are man-made. Repenting certainly involves moving away from past errors, inherited from our fathers which are of no profit. Excusing errors in the traditional teachings of men is where Yahushua Himself was most critical of the Torah-teachers of 2000 years ago. The "restoration of all things" involves removing the human traditions, and restoring the Commandments of YHWH. "Overcoming" the traditions is not easy, and the made-up name "Jesus" is simply of human origin. I feel Yahushua will bring all those whose hearts are pure to Himself in the last day. If we hold grudges, and insist on what we have decided is "perfection" in those we associate with, then we may be in for a rude awakening.

We are our own worst enemy sometimes because we try too hard and strain to get the details correct, but miss the big picture -- it's only about love. I've seen people develop under the guidance of Messianic pastors, and they get so involved in keeping hair, arms, and legs covered that they are in worse bondage than humans can bear up under. Cleaning the outside of the cup is doing nothing; a white-washed tomb is just for show. Developing Statements of faith that basically exclude all other believers who may be slightly different (because they may observe the moon as a crescent or black ball, or some other difference), sometimes cause confrontations and divisions within the Body. Such things are "shadows" of what is to come. Personally, I believe it's possible that some "Sun-day" - keepers will be in the world-to-come, because even though they had many things wrong in their training they could rise above their petty pride and accept others in love, and in their hearts they love YHWH. They don't know what's wrong or right yet, so have no sin. It's when they learn the Truth that they become responsible for it. Yahushua is Truth personified, and He realizes that each of us is a work in progress -- our problem is we don't seem to be conscious of that fact very often in our personal lives, and as we watch others work out their salvation. To me love is the highest calling we must commit ourselves to. Being right about every detail isn't going to earn us any points, but loving others enough to accept them with their flaws is the greatest test of our true nature. If Yahushua loved them, while still in their sins, enough to be nailed to wood -- then the least we can do is have a little courtesy and patience ourselves. The Yahushua I know isn't the type that writes people off very easily. If they are chosen, He will wait and continue to work on them.

If you looked at the 9 fruits of the Spirit and tried to imagine what their "opposites" might be, you'd see the traits of the mind of the flesh. The fruit of the Spirit consists of: LOVE - JOY - PEACE - PATIENCE - KINDNESS - GOODNESS - GENTLENESS - FAITHFULNESS - & SELF CONTROL. The world without Torah produces hate, despair, war, ruthlessness, and the like. Basically, sin is hatred; hatred of YHWH, and hatred of our neighbor (produced by pride, and selfishness). Read Philippians 4:5-8, and you'll see how Yahushua views our world, and we strive to imitate Him. If we simply "do what Yahushua would do", we probably won't be too far off the correct path.

Q: Regarding Peoples of different races; African, Indian, and Asian Peoples,how do you believe they fit into Yahweh's plan? Can they be truly saved? Can they claim all the same promises as White Anglo Saxons?

Answer: I believe I've already answered this above. Yes, the verses at Yesha Yahu 56 clearly guarantee that all nations will be granted the right to YHWH's mountain, and at verse 6 He *ties* it to keeping from profaning *His Sabbaths*, and holding to His Covenant. I'm "white"; I understand genetics enough to realize that white people have *lost* genetic information just as the polar bear has -- the black bear is the same animal, but contains *more information*. Over time, each generation loses genetic information. It's my belief that Adam and Chuwah were very black, Noach was an albino, and the races of Negroid, Mongoloid, and Caucasoid all came about through Noach's three sons Shem, Ham, and Yapheth. White people have lost genetic information; their melonin content is severely lacking. It was slowly bred-out, most likely because populations became isolated. The original human had to have had a very black complexion. Ham was black, and Cush was of his lineage; Cushites are black (Acts 8:27), and so are Ethiopians (Jer. 13:23). This distinction was troublesome to "racists" even in the time of Mosheh (Num. 12:1), but we must remember whichever race we are, if we view other races with disdain, WE JUDGE THEIR MAKER, and this puts us in a very precarious position -- YHWH could strike us with leprosy for it as He did Mosheh's sister, Miryam. Then your skin would be so hideous, you'd gladly become whatever race in exchange for your problem. We are truly evil in our hearts, but Yahushua wants us to see ourselves as He sees us - in love, great enough to lay our lives down for one another. Being a living sacrifice is better.

Q: What about intermarrying of people of different races?

Answer: Interracial marriage! I know that there are those who teach against this practice, and even Mosheh was criticized for being married to a black girl -- (Num. 12:1) -- but this was shown to be wrong to criticize. This circumstance would also indicate that Mosheh was not black. When we "rank" ourselves or judge the worthiness of others based on any external trait, we judge their Maker, and this is also taken as a personal insult to Him. The 3 primary races on this planet are the descendants of Shem, Ham, and Yapheth. These three brothers along with their wives provided all the human genetic material we see in the world today. In a few moments you'll gain some insight into what's been happening between the races, from a genetic viewpoint. After you comprehend my reasoning, you'll understand completely why I'm not "prejudiced" toward other races. Although I'm a Caucasoid, I love the Orientals and Cushites and have no superiority complex or racial bias. If anything, I feel inferior because I'm not "racially mixed" -- and there is a genetic basis for this. The fact that we even need to ask the question about whether intermarrying between races is appropriate is an indication that we have been influenced by social attitudes implanted into our thinking through cultural biases. Personally, I feel the offspring of inter-racial couples are BEAUTIFUL people; and in just a few moments you'll understand why. The races (Negroid, Caucasoid, Mongoloid) can be viewed to be "breeds" of human beings, similar to the way we think of the "breeds" of cats, dogs, and other living species. "Breeding" also means "selecting" - and what is selected are "traits", which appear as dominant when other dominant traits are taken away, or selected-out. You see, our DNA contains an enormous amount of *information*; and it is either "on" or "off" -- but it's still there. When a gene is switched "on", this means the trait is expressed, such as hair or eye color, or whatever trait the gene controls. Our traits arise from genetic information in our DNA, manifesting a diversity of dominant characteristics -- but we are all of the same blood, and origin, and have 46 chromosomes. The idea of "cross-breeding" arises from a mistaken assumption; if we interbreed the races, we are really restoring and re-combining what had been separated-out. Greyhound dogs and wolves are the same *species*, it's just that the Greyhound has lost a great deal of genetic information, by "breeding-out" that information, not breeding more in! If I were in the market to remarry, I'm sure I'd be attracted to a woman who had a balanced genetic background from all 3 races, more so than from being genetically isolated to one of the races. Our thinking is so confused, we have made up terms like "half-breed" and "mutt" to describe the re-blending of the DNA content to the original, restoring that which was lost. Genetically, intermarrying is the best thing that could possibly happen; but we have to overcome the mental blocks, and de-program the cultural errors of millennia.

I feel that Paul's advice for us to "test ourselves" to make sure we were in the faith is good advice. As long as we avoid using our diverse "statements of faith" as reasons for divisions, I feel they are justified. I don't hang my "list" in others' faces, and I am also prepared to repent of any beliefs I hold that are in error. Sin is not just being wrong, it's hatred -- of YHWH, and our fellow mankind. We can claim to be a follower of Yahushua, but by our actions we can deny Him. When we love YHWH and our fellow mankind, we have fulfilled the Torah. The media programs our minds in subtle ways, and is constantly steering our culture. Currently it is also being steered toward witchcraft, and promotes "toleration" of all sorts of abominations -- but "toleration" of the Truth (such as Intelligent Design, or obedience to the Ten Commandments) is hardly seen. "For rebellion is as the sin of divination, and stubbornness is as wickedness and idolatry." (1 Sam. 15:23). The public schools/textbooks, libraries, book distribution, and general media (radio, TV, magazines, newspapers) have positioned people in specific positions to block Truth. They allow Satanic and corrupt programming/ printing to disseminate into the culture, in order to CHANGE

THE CULTURE into what they want it to be.

STATEMENT OF FAITH

Based on, and in accord with, the Statement of Faith of the
Union of Two House Messianic Congregations

I believe that YHWH is the only living Elohim, and that He is One. (Hear, O Yisrael, YHWH is our Elohim; YHWH is ONE!).

I believe the oracles of YHWH were given to Israel, and preserved by them as a witness to the Truth.

I believe YHWH is the Creator of all things seen and unseen, and from this Spirit proceeds all matter, life, energy, and existence.

I believe that Yahushua is the only begotten Son of YHWH, Who came in the flesh by the sovereign power of YHWH of a virgin, died, resurrected, ascended, and now awaits His return to possess the Kingdom. His Spirit indwells those in the New Covenant now, and He is seeking out the lost sheep of the House of Israel, and drawing many foreigners to be obedient to the Covenant. These "lost sheep" are the prodigal son from the parable. (The "older brother" in the parable represents Yahudah, or the tribe called "Jews", who stubbornly remained with the Father in His Covenant, although they broke it). I love my brothers, the Yahudim.That in Yahushua dwells all the fullness of omnipotence, and that YHWH and His Messiah/Savior are both YHWH (Colossians 2:9).

I believe that YHWH is rescuing from the nations and false religions, a redeemed blood-washed remnant by Yahushua's blood, and rebuilding ALL Israel. Renewed-Covenant Israel is defined as Judah (Yahudah) and Ephraim, the **two houses** becoming one again, through our Messiah Yahushua. Their companions are the minority non-Israelites, who by Messiah's atonement, join the nation of Israel, and become Israel but are not "Jews" in the sense of bloodline.

We recognize that all Jews (Yahudim) are Israelites but also that all Israelites are not Yahudim (the other 10 tribes are "Samaritans", because they are dispersed from "Samaria") -- First Peter 2:9, Ezekiel 37:16.

I believe that through the **two-house restoration**, both houses are having their blinders removed. Yahudah needs

Messiah and Ephraim needs Torah, and their identity as Israel's other house restored (Isaiah 8:14).

I believe that all believers in Messiah Yahshua are *Israel*, regardless of whether they come from Yahudah, Ephraim (10 tribes), or have no Israelite blood, but have *joined* Israel's Commonwealth through submission to Israel's King Messiah Yahshua. Thus the ekklessia / kahal is *Israel restored* (Ephesians 2:11-19).

I believe that the so-called 'church' does not exist apart from the historic people of *Israel*, and as such never replaced Jewish-Israel as Israel (Acts 7:38, Acts 2: 1-47).

I reject all forms or derivations of *Replacement Theology*. Jewish-Israel's major covenants with YHWH are eternal and unconditional (Jer. 31:33-34).

I believe that the only true eternal personal Names of the Father and the Son are Yahuah and the Son Yahushua (or Yahshua). While the spelling is not important, the usage is.

I believe that only the precious, set apart blood of the Lamb of YHWH, Yahushua, can totally remove and remit one's sins. John 1:29

I believe that both *Replacement Theology*, (where something man-made called "The Church" replaces the Jews) and *Separate Entity Theology*, (where something man-made called "The Church" co-exists as a separate "Spiritual-Israel" entity alongside the people of physical Jewish-Israel) are both *unscriptural doctrines* and need to be silenced via correct teaching by those of the single body of New Covenant Israel, also known as the ecclesia the Assembly of Yahshua. Israel can only be defined, as those who are physical human beings, with a physical connection to Israel, along with a spiritual connection to Israel by being born again believers on and in Yahushua of Nazareth - Ephesians 2:11-19. They OBEY the Covenant Ten Commandments, or else are cut-off from Israel. Most of the "lost sheep" are in Christian denominations today, and many are awakening to their calling to return. Like the prodigal, they are "coming to their senses", and realizing who they are, and why they are finding they love Israel -- they are aware that they ARE Israel. They are finding they love the Torah, and are learning what the New Covenant really is. That Ephraim's recognition of their identity and restoration with brother Judah is the truth that will become the salvation of all Israel in the millennial (Ezekiel 37:16-28, Romans 11:25-26).

I believe that Yahushua's physical return to earth will result in the ultimate restoration of the Kingdom to Israel (Acts 1:6), as He takes both "sticks" of Ezekiel 37 and makes them one in YHWH's hand on the mountains of Israel, as all Israel is saved, **honoring Yahushua**, **obeying Torah**, and enjoying the restoration of David's Tabernacle which had previously fallen.

I'm opposed to any sects of White-Aryan Ephraimitism, or anything remotely anti-Jewish, anti-Israel, anti Zionist or that can be construed as being anti-Semitic. Most British-Israel groups are also considered outside the realm of membership for some of the same reasons mentioned above.

I believe salvation and eternal life is only through Yahushua, and can be attained by being **convicted of one's sins** by hearing the Word (Torah, Covenant, Commandments), then **repenting**, and being **immersed in the Name of Yahushua of Natsarith**, and continuing on living in the way shown by the Torah -- without sin. The New Covenant is having one's heart **circumcised** by Yahushua's Spirit, so that the Commandments are written on our hearts (Yerme Yahu 31:31, Hebrew 8). Our **immersion** symbolizes this circumcision. Yahushua's message/testimony of the Kingdom is: **"Repent, for the reign of YHWH draws near."** His followers teach others to love YHWH, love one's neighbor, and love one's enemies. The keep the Commandments of YHWH, **and** hold to the testimony of Yahushua. Sin is hatred of YHWH, and hatred of one's neighbor.

I believe that a person can claim to **believe** in and be a follower of Yahushua, but by their **actions** they can deny Him.

Wrong name, yet *miracles*

A simple question is regularly asked, and it has to have an answer. A sister wrote it this way:

Shalom, brother Lew,

There is a close friend of mine who questions why Yahuah and His Son would answer Christians when they are invoking the pagan names. I have taught her from Scripture about many things, which she is trying to follow, like eating kosher, keeping Sabbath, and honoring our Elohim with the True Names (Yahuah, Yahushua). She watched a program recently, where Christians testified of some great miracles and, of course, they all called on the wrong names. She cannot understand why Yahuah would honor their petitions.

My humble understanding as I shared with her, is that He is so merciful that He wants to send help to those whose hearts are trying to address the Almighty, even when using the wrong names. But this does not minister to her.

Dear sister,

People will be asking this question until Yahushua returns. The real answer to it is the simple fact that you've already arrived at. What would Yahushua say if anyone came to Him and asked it? Possibly, He would ask another question.

It might be a question something like:

"Why do you resist accepting My true Name?"

They are only responsible when they have been told, and to reject the Truth is what will bring upon them serious consequences. We were told we would be hated, and one reason was over His Name. Yahushua once said,

"If the world hates you, keep in mind that it hated me first. If you belonged to the world, it would love you as its own. As it is, you do not belong to the world, but I have chosen you out of the world. That is why the world hates you. Remember the words I spoke to you: ' No servant is greater than his master.' If they persecuted me, they will persecute you also. If they obeyed my teaching, they will obey (LISTEN TO) **yours also. They will treat you this way because of My Name, for they do not know the One who sent me** (THEY DON'T KNOW HIS NAME)**. If I had not come and spoken to them, they would not be guilty of sin. Now, however, they have no excuse for their sin. He who hates me hates my Father as well. If I had not done among them what no one else did, they would not be guilty of sin. But now they have seen these miracles, and yet they have hated both me and my Father. But this is to fulfill what is written in their Law: 'They hated me without reason.'"** John / Yahuchanon 15:18-25

"I tell you the truth, My Father will give you whatever you ask in My Name. Until now you have not asked for

anything in My Name. Ask and you will receive, and your joy will be complete." John / Yahuchanon 16:23-24

These verses could be used to support the false name, but only until it is realized through personal **study** that the true Name was exchanged for the false one. When anyone uses the false name, they do it in innocently. They are not responsible *until they are told.* Even though the adversary would have it blotted-out forever if possible, those who the Mashiach reveals Himself to will know and love His true, and only Name. "JESUS" has no meaning in Hebrew. Yahushua means **"Yah - is our - salvation".** **Signs** and **wonders** are only for a wicked, rebellious generation - but we walk by our faith (emunah). Rather than just trying to prove that "JESUS" is His true Name, by Jesuit logic (only looking at the Greek texts), we need to understand that "YAH" is contained in the Name, and isn't there in the Latinized-Greek name.

Another incredible mind-numbing realization awaits all Christians: We are **engrafted** into the **commonwealth of Israel** - we don't "replace" Israel. We have no business **labeling** ourselves with a Greek term either; we're **"Natsarim"** (Acts 24:5). The article at www.fossilizedcustoms.com/christian.html may shed light on what is wrong with using "kristos" to describe those who are following the Messiah of Israel. Greek we don't need! To attempt to justify anything pertaining to His Name or His title using Greek is the height of desperation, and **absurd.** *Objectively, take the name "James". Etymologists and theologians alike all agree it was originally the Hebrew name "Ya'aqob". Yet, for some reason, we see a cultural stubbornness, sometimes evoking a rage, over the true, original Name of the Mashiach of Israel.* There is probably a **demonic spell** or **stronghold** associated with the name of error. People will accept the false name much more readily than the one TRUE NAME; this is exactly what Yahushua *said* would happen:

"I have come in my Father's Name, and you do not accept me; but if someone else comes in his own name, you will accept him." John / Yahuchanon 5:43-44

Now, watch the following verses carefully, because they reveal the **reason** for being condemned:

"For [Elohim] *so loved the world that he gave His one and only Son, that whoever believes in Him shall not perish but have eternal life. For* [Elohim] *did not send His Son into the world to condemn the world, but to save the world through Him. Whoever believes in Him is not condemned, but whoever does not believe stands condemned already because he has not believed in the <u>Name</u> of* [Eloah's] *one and only Son."* John / Yahuchanon 3:16-18

"Salvation is found in no one else, for there is no other name under heaven given to men by which we must be saved." Acts 4:12

Rebellion is as the sin of witchcraft, so we don't want to rebel against YHWH. We can rebel against *human traditions* however, and that is the source of most doctrinal con-

THE DAWN OF THE NEW WORLD ORDER:

UNITED NATIONS WORLD TYRANNY

2001 A Space Odyssey monolith

UN Building, New York City (right)

flicts. You can lead a horse to water, but you can't make him drink. The solution is not to fight about it, but be patient. Your close friend is dealing with the fact that she is inside a "box", and you are outside that box communicating and revealing extremely challenging information. She is at a critical point, as we were all there at one time. Let her study Scripture to prove you wrong, and she will find her way, guided by Yahushua's Spirit. One last comment; when we witness or hear of a miraculous event, we should withhold our opinion on the matter as being "from the evil one", since if it *is in fact* an act of the Ruach ha'Qodesh, we have committed an *unpardonable offense*. The motivation of the people involved may be unworthy, however Yahushua still performs miracles. It is a sign of little faith in those who must seek after a sign, and any person who uses miracles as a means to gain riches has certainly received their reward in full. No further reward will be given to them. But, even if for the wrong intention a wonderful miracle occurs, the *Mashiach is preached*:

"The former preach Messiah out of selfish ambition, not sincerely, supposing that they can stir up trouble for me while I am in chains. But what does it matter? The important thing is that in every way, whether from false motives or true, Messiah is preached . And because of this I rejoice." Phil 1:17-18

Upon learning the true Name, a sincere, humble person would go to the waters of immersion again, and call on the only Name given among men for salvation: **YAHUSHUA**. Let the nations rage against the Mashiach, and take counsel together; Yahuah will speak to them in His wrath (Ps. 2).

"Who has established all the ends of the Earth? What is His Name, and what is His Son's name , if you know?" Prov 30:4

The Agenda

The **New World** (Jesuit) **Order** & World Tyranny

"The Agenda" is one term for the "new world order" used by the insiders / globalists -- the ILLUMINISTS, also called the ILLUMINATI. Ultimately, the "agenda" is: *to move the Papacy to Jerusalem* - this has been the primary design for

1600 years, *only overshadowed by the objective to wipe out the entire nation of Israel from the Earth*. This conspiracy is very old, and of course is also known as the "hidden agenda". Think about history; Constantine moved the capital of the empire eastward from Rome, to "Constantinople" (**this one move was about 2/3 of the way**). This was one of the first major leaps to achieve *The Agenda*. What a goof it turned out to be; it was probably one of the *real* major reasons for the fall of the empire within a few decades. All the *roads* of the empire led to *Rome*, not Constantinople, so the authoritarian rule could no longer be sustained. The barbarians swept into the abandoned city of Rome. The totalitarian grip of the "Nicolaitans" (Catholic Papist tyrants) had to re-group; not long afterward they were slapped in the face with the "*Magna Carta*", or "Great Charter", *defining* and *limiting* the powers of rulers. They've designed conflicts of every sort, and even invented Islam to plow the way for the big Papal move from Rome to Jerusalem. When it failed to achieve the goals it was designed for, 400 years of "Crusades" were sent against the new invaders of Jerusalem. No matter what they did, the Papacy could not seem to get moved to Jerusalem.

When Israel was established in 1948, *The Agenda* became endangered of never becoming possible. The friendship of Israel and the US is their open sore, *and they bewail it at every turn*, especially in their own halls of the *United Nations*. The ultimate charter to control power-lusting rulers is embodied in the *US Constitution*. It is designed to *control government*, not citizens. It sets boundaries of behavior and limits the powers of government, so the **US Constitution** is like KRYPTONITE to tyrannical Papists -- they want to *destroy it*. They keep calling for a "new constitutional convention". The U.S. Constitution will NEVER allow a *concordat* to be established with the Papacy. It empowers the people, not their "god", the Pope. The Pope *rules* over the leaders of the nations of this world, and to back up that claim we simply look at Rev. 18:3, but it's best to read chapters 17 & 18 entirely. Daniel 4:17 tells us that we are ruled over by the lowest of men; that's religiously and politically. The Jesuit JEDI are also controlling the media. They are phenomenal propagandists. After all, the Jesuits put the finishing touches on the Roman calendar we all inherited from Julius Caesar;

They are also the source of the promoted name, "JESUS", which many are now learning is not the true *"one Name given among men by which we must be saved"*. They are known as "*The Society of Jesus*", and also promote the "inspired Greek New Covenant". They promote "Mary-worship", because their founder, Inigo de Loyola, was obsessed with Yahushua's mother. Their influence around the world through seminaries is one thing; but they also play a part in every social and political upheaval wherever they may occur. Often a media person will interview a "Jesuit priest"; but be aware, they are all Jesuit priests, even those in deep cover within societies -- they are the primary agitators to change or over-throw regimes. They are rampant in the media (broadcasting, print, etc.,.) The nerve-center to watch is the **UNITED NATIONS**. Created by the **CFR** (Illuminati), the UN is the "New World Order", and will be firmly established as the one-world government when the *globalists* set up the UN TAX they have planned for every person on Earth. The **Secret Order of the Quest** (world domination, NWO) is planned and facilitated ultimately by:

The Jesuits: *Assassins, Teachers, Infiltrators, Tyrants*

They are in fact fascists. The head of the Nazi SS was the Jesuit priest, "father Himmler", who modeled the SS after the Jesuit Order. The UN is their organization. These two pictures literally illustrate what is happening. In the movie 2001 A Space Odyssey, the apes represent free men; but one morning they wake up and their "country" was taken over by the presence of a foreign object - forever changed! Have you ever felt that your country is no longer the same one you were born in?

The US Constitution is their primary obstacle, and it is under constant attack by infiltrating CFR members as "candidates" for US government offices 24/7. Proclaiming "liberty" as a right of all people means tyrants can't go around locking-up people without due process. They have a right to their liberty -- personal freedom to travel and live where they choose. This was not so until the US Constitution declared it. They (tyrannical Papists) tried their hand at global domination with the "League of Nations", and it failed. A few decades later, they tried it again with a new name, the United Nations, and it's about to work. They even placed its headquarters in the US, their greatest obstacle to their success, with the hope that becoming a recognized "fixture" will make us more comfortable having them around. The UN is a foreign power on US soil. New York and Chicago are the most populous Catholic areas in the USA. The ILLUMINATI changed its name to operate as a "shadow government" within the US government through the infiltration of its members -- it is known as **CFR**, or the Council on Foreign Relations. The Jesuits are fantastic infiltrators. Another element of the "shadow government" is the **Central Bank**, called the "FED", or "Federal Reserve Bank". The Catholic-Jesuit-CFR-FED infestation within the US government is "cloaked" almost as if people are unaware of what they are really looking at. "**Maryland**", the state, is named for "Mary"; the Whitehouse is built on farmland that was originally named "**Rome**". Those who you would never consider to be "Catholic" would surprise you -- once Jesuit-trained, they enter their disguised, infiltrating role and often seem to be against Catholicism. You would not believe the list of men who are Jesuit-trained

(do a search on google using the key words "Jesuit trained"; Francis Cardinal Spellman, Fidel Castro, Adam Weishaupt, Cecil Rhodes, -- and many others that would shock you, like Yassar Arafat).   The organization, the **CFR**, _is_ the Illuminati, in disguise.   Presidents from _both sides of the aisle_ are elected from its membership; so effectively there is really only ONE party, the CFR.   The parties are simply different "management teams".   Whichever one "wins" in any election, POLICY doesn't change one wit.   "Democrat" or "Republican" -- such labels are meaningless really, because the outcome of either winning an election will be the same.   The objectives of the CFR will be carried out.   Their main purse strings extend from the central bank, the Federal Reserve Bank (a private bank, but it has an "official" sounding name).   They thrive financially on our national debt.   Follow the money-trail, and you'll find the really bad-guys.   The Jesuits.   Sure, they use the ruse or facade of "Jewish bankers" to hide behind, but this is all propaganda.   "Blame it on the Jews" is their excuse every time.   Forget about the "Rothchilds" --

that's all just FORD/NAZI propaganda promoted through the "Protocols of the Elders of Zion" non-sense.   The *"Protocols of the Elders of Zion"* is actually a *Jesuit-authored* forgery authorized by the anti-Semitic Czarist police in early 20th-Century Russia that *purports* to be minutes of a meeting of top Jewish leaders plotting world domination.   The Jesuits composed the "*Protocols*", and in fact many of them wear their own Jesuit protocols written in a miniature book on a chain around their necks.   These little books contain the Jesuit protocols, which the Jesuits used as the *model* for the "Protocols of the Elders of Zion".   The Jesuits coined the word "Zionism".   Henry Ford had this Jesuit-authored document translated into English and published in America, but it was all composed by Jesuits as a conspiracy to "frame" the Yahudim for their own actions.   Hitler had a portrait of Henry Ford behind his desk, declaring that

"this is one American who understands us".

Vatican / Jesuit assassins have killed many;   Abraham Lincoln, the Czar of Russia and his family, and John F. Kennedy to name but a few.   The *Order* (Jesuits) were at the center of the Vietnam conflict, as they used the Catholic president (Diem) of South Vietnam to wipe out the Buddhists. You'll notice the Jesuits are present in most of the conflicts around the world.   Often, the media interviews them, and even tells you they are "Jesuit priests".   Over the centuries, they would get as close to leaders as possible, and become their advisors.   They would teach the leaders' children, and the higher classes' children, in order to steer the culture toward the Papacy.   The illustration here shows an overview of their current international organizational structure.

Here's a few words shared from www.deoxy.org:

*"The head of the global banking trans-corporation known as the Illuminati is in Belgium, at the famous **Castle of Darkness**, a large mansion estate in the countryside near Muno. The Illuminati are actually the JESUITS (remember the Spanish Inquisition?) they have never disappeared from the Earth, they are the modern Elite EU banking families we have today. (Rothchilds,bank of London, etc.,.) They control most of the politicians in Belgium and the USA through Blackmail and Coercion-tactics, including sexual blackmail, death threats, etc.*

The **Castle of Darkness** is a real castle in MUNO, BELGIUM, in case you want to run an internet search.

Muno, Belgium is famous for its JESUIT roots, and many JESUITS still live in the area today. The JESUITS are obsessed with global domination and have been at it for many centuries. They are all over the world, and practice ancient SAXON BLOOD RITES and RITUALS, that include child sacrifice to satan. Run a search on google for **"Belgium's silent heart of darkness"**. The URL: http://observer.guardian.co.uk/review/story/0,6903,710090,00.html -You will see a pattern of kidnapped children, terrified Judges, and dead witnesses surrounding the JESUITS and evidence of ritual satanic torture and murder, etc., wherever they hold their secret meetings, many local kidnapped children are never seen alive again. (on December 16, 2004, a woman was killed and her baby cut from her womb in Missouri, USA, and there have been many other women killed and their babies taken from their wombs).

The Illuminati are the brains behind the NEW WORLD ORDER, and have a global plan for its conception and design.
Many of the former US presidents are members of their secret society, they meet in America at a place in Northern California called **BOHEMIAN GROVE**. Run a search of Google for BOHEMIAN GROVE. Alex Jones made a secret video of the Bohemian Grove meetings (Near Monte Rio California) where you can see the JESUIT Rituals being performed next to a giant stone statue of **HORUS** the Falcon. The JESUITS secretly hold Egyptian statues in high esteem to be used in some of the outdoor rituals." (end of excerpt)

The Jesuit General is often called "the black pope". Truly, whoever this man happens to be at any point in time, he's the most powerful man on Earth. They will use some "Latin" because any good old-school Catholic knows this is a "sacred" language. Actually, Latin is the language of the men who executed our Messiah, Yahushua -- the Italian Roman army (it wasn't carried out by the "Jews" after all, but the Romans). Watch for the Latin stuff -- they use it to hide meanings from the common, uninitiated population. Also, remember there is "old Latin" and "new Latin" -- words are spelled slightly differently, and this allows them to further conceal their cryptic messages to one another.

"Announcing the birth of a new world order." These words are inscribed on the back of each US Dollar bill, written in Latin: ***ANNUIT COEPTIS NOVUS ORDO SECLORUM.*** The "ORDER" that is being described here, to cut-to-the-chase, is the JESUIT ***ORDER***. To conceal the true meaning of the words, this "motto" is translated for ***public consumption*** in a number of benign-sounding ways: in their words, as it is now translated by the U.S. State Department: *"He (God) has favored our undertakings."*

The ***disinformation*** concerning these words written on the "Great Seal" is very strange, and it's possible there are people gullible enough to believe it. Thomson coined the motto: Novus ordo seclorum. For example, they "translate" (twist) the phrase ***NOVUS ORDO SECLORUM*** this way:

The *accepted* translation is: ***A new order of the ages.*** (notice the word "accepted").

Thomson explained:
"The date underneath [the pyramid] is that of the Declaration of Independence and the words under it signify the beginning of the new American Æra, which commences from that date."
THEY NOTE: *"'Novus ordo seclorum' cannot translate into 'new world order.'"* - Uh-huh . . . right. *Disinformation!*

The Illuminati and the Free Masons adhere to the hope that eventually the ***"New World Order"*** will be ushered in, and they will be the puppet masters. They believe their "arcane" and mysterious secrets will draw men to them; Adam Weishaupt actually stated that it was the "mystery" of his organization that made it so easy to control people. Men don't learn this at the lower levels, but Masonic authors writing to their own brotherhood of "masters" have revealed that they worship Osiris / Horus, and this is why the ***Great Seal*** has the "EYE" at the top of the Egyptian pyramid. It's Horus, one of the many names for satan. They admit the name changes according to the culture; but ultimately it is the sun, and "Lucifer" that they call upon with the name "JA-BUL-ON" (a combining of the name YHWH, BAAL, and ON).

The familiar logo we call the "Great Seal" was really adopted from the Illuminati, and its designer was actually Adam Weishaupt of Bavaria, the Illuminati's founder (a Jesuit). He founded the Illuminati in 1776, seen in ROMAN nu-

Joseph Ratzinger (78) assumed the title *"Pontifex Maximus"* on Roman Date 4-19-2005 - a title which began in *46 BCE!* He is now going by "Pope Benedict XVI" in costume.

merals at the base of the Nimrod-pyramid-obelisk seen on every one dollar bill.   The glowing EYE is not YHWH, but rather satan, worshipped for millennia as the SUN.   The "eye-in-the-sky" has always been the sun, called Solis Invictus, Horus, Molech, to just name a few.   The occultic (hidden) religion of the Pagan king NIMROD is secretly being kept alive through traditions, and secret societies all over the globe.   Is there any doubt in anyone's mind that the fabulous "builders", the Masons, might not be involved to some extent?   The Jesuits are the ultimate control freaks, or tyrants, and have been attacking our rule of law, the US Constitution, for 200 years.   They assassinated Abraham Lincoln because he resisted the establishment of a "central bank".   The Jesuit assassins murdered him.   The Jesuits cannot operate with a free hand as long as the US Constitution is controlling their actions.   The US Constitution grants and defends life, liberty (non-imprisonment), and the pursuit of happiness to all men, as inalienable rights endowed to them by the Creator.   It only limits and controls GOVERNMENT, and shuts down their authoritarian, oppressive, invasive tyrannical tendencies.   Politicians serving the interests of the Jesuit Order have for years attempted to change, bend, and stretch the US Constitution in order to free their hands and get at us.

The government of the United States derives its power from the consent of the governed, and all men are created equal.   (Not "evolved" equally, but created).   The first thing they do when they take their oath of office is swear to defend the US Constitution, but they break this oath often, and get away with it.   It has been said, *When the government is afraid, there is justice and liberty;   when the people are*

Peter Hans Kolvenbach - General of the Jesuits
ROMANISM IS SYNONOMOUS WITH FASCISM

afraid, there is tyranny. Yes, the US Constitution leaves no room for tyrants to take control -- and tyranny is the main goal of the JESUIT ORDER. It seems that the only people who study the U.S. Constitution are new immigrants; we free persons hardly ever see it. If you were to read it right now, your heart would burn within you. You would know how much it has been over-stepped. A similar thing happened to someone long ago concerning the eternal Covenant:

"When the king heard the words of the Book of the Law (Torah scroll)*, he tore his robes . He gave these orders to HilkiYah the priest, Ahikam son of Shaphan, Acbor son of MicaYah, Shaphan the secretary and AsaYah the king's attendant: 'Go and inquire of the Yahuah for me and for the people and for all Yahudah about what is written in this book that has been found. Great is Yahuah's anger that burns against us because our fathers have not obeyed the words of this book; they have not acted in accordance with all that is written there concerning us.'"*
2 Kings 22:11-13

Through free public education, Humanism is promoted (an atheist religion promoting situation ethics). The conspiracy of the globalistic Jesuit/Illuminists is to establish a world government (U.N.) by "educating" the children with evolution-communism-Humanism ideals, and have the nations of the Earth submit to the global laws, and slowly surrender their arms in exchange for the military protection of the World Government.   The objective is world peace, accomplished by the "peace keepers", the U.N. strike forces.   The **_Humanist Manifesto_** reveals the ultimate objectives of the new world order, and seeks to eliminate the family unit and all competing religions.

There has been a constant attack against the US Constitution, the rule of Law we are ruled by in our Republic.   The average person hears "democracy" so often, they accept it.   The Nazi party (NSDAP) was made up of social democrats.   Candidates, presidents, and the media use the word democracy sometimes correctly, that is when they describe the process used in electing those who represent us.   Our form of government, however, is not a democracy; it is a republican form of government, and that government is controlled and kept in check by the rule of law, the US Constitution.   "We the people" are the government, and we elect those who represent our will, so those governed over allow and consent to the policies of that government.   As the world grows increasingly reprobate morally, we witness scandalous behavior at every level of society.   Yahushua will rescue His pious ones from what is coming, and fire will consume every abomination.

The majority doesn't rule over our people, the rule of Law does, expressed in the US Constitution and Bill of Rights.   The majority simply elects our representatives, who are elected to defend the US Constitution.

George Washington warned us long ago:

"Government is not reason; it is not eloquent; it is force.
Like fire, it is a dangerous servant and a fearful master."

If we were ruled by what the majority wanted, we would be a mob-ruled nation.   Or, we would be ruled over by the tyranny of a papist, as most of the countries of Europe we escaped from have been (investigate the word "concordat").   A papist is a patsy of the "Pope", whether they be ruling a country or simply obeying Roman Church "dogma".   Persecution of any minority is not justice, and cannot lead to peace.   We are seeing the last days of the US Constitution now, and soon authoritarian, tyrannical billionaire-lawyers will enslave us even more through higher taxation, national debt, high interest rates, and national emergencies engineered by Jesuit manipulation. High courts are misinterpreting the Constitution, which was instituted for the sole purpose of controlling the government, not the citizens. Courts are molding LAWS through their twisted decisions, countering what legislators have established. Ultimately, the force behind this activism in the judges must be: JESUITS. When time permits, do a Google-search on the words: Jesuit assassins.

All small businesses will be out-lawed, and Socialism will grow in demand, to attempt to solve all the problems for the citizens.

The military industrial complex, and the shadow government guided by the CFR, have already entrenched themselves (infiltration), but the population doesn't realize it yet. The "Order" in the phrase "New World Order" is really the Jesuit Order, which uses the central bank (Federal Reserve) to fill its treasuries. With wealth and power, there is nothing they cannot accomplish. They control where and when The Scriptures may be quoted in public; and soon they will out-law possessing them, since the new laws concerning "hate crimes" will enable them to do so. This will not be the first time the RCC outlawed the possession of the Scriptures;

THE GEORGIA GUIDESTONES

among the "dogmas" (official teachings) of the Roman Church, you will find that in 1229 the Scriptures were forbidden to all "laymen". This is against Yn. 5:39, 8:31, and 2 Tim. 3:15-17. The vast majority of the "priests" of Catholicism were not permitted to read Scripture -- they truly were the **"Dark Ages"** between Constantine and the Reformation, simply because Catholicism had the world in a fascist head-lock.

There's quite a bit more to consider. There's a separating taking place between the sheep and the goats, between the two world-views. The Ten Commandments display was removed from the Alabama Supreme Court building. There was a good reason for the removing them:
"You can't post **Thou Shalt Not Steal, Thou Shalt Not Commit Adultery and Thou Shall Not Lie**, in a building full of politicians and lawyers without creating a hostile work environment." ---- from anonymous Email

Joseph Ratzinger (78) assumed the title "Pontifex Maximus" on Roman Date 4-19-2005 - a title which began in 46 BCE!
now going by "Pope Benedict XVI" in costume. He leads the Curia, the same organization the Pontifex Maximus of Roma set up under the sun-worshipping Caesars. Many of the same statues used by the Pagan Mithraic culture have been re-named. Not only are statues/images used, but also many other Pagan articles: holy water, medals, scapulars, steeples, bells, rosaries, candles, costumes, the Kyrie Eleison, the calendar, solar-shaped wreaths, domes, relics, crosses, and former Pagan feast dates revised to put a Scriptural spin on

Murderers can identify one another easily, as we see here.
Saddam, Inigo, and Adolf: ALL THREE MEN HAVE HATED ONE GROUP OF PEOPLE. CAN YOU GUESS WHAT GROUP THAT IS?

things, blending the Satanic model with new terms and meanings. "Ishtar" became "Easter", and the "birth of the Sun" became Christmas. The solar image, the crux, became the central symbol of Christianity during the 4th century. Most Jesuits, if not all, know all these things. They simply keep it from becoming popular knowledge. This "pope" is also known within Catholicism as:

"Governor of the World" and ***"God on Earth"***
(To Catholics, according to their Dogma)
whose master is:

Peter Hans Kolvenbach
General of the Jesuits
Sovereign over the Pope   "PAPA NERO", OR BLACK POPE

From www.infoplease.com, we read this about
The Dead Sea Scrolls:

Discovery of the Scrolls

"The first of the Dead Sea Scroll discoveries occurred in 1947 in Qumran, a village situated about twenty miles east of Jerusalem on the northwest shore of the Dead Sea. A young Bedouin shepherd, following a goat that had gone astray, tossed a rock into one of the caves along the seacliffs and heard a cracking sound: the rock had hit a ceramic pot containing leather and papyrus scrolls that were later determined to be nearly twenty centuries old. Ten years and many searches later, eleven caves around the Dead Sea were found to contain tens of thousands of scroll fragments dating from the third century B.C. to A.D. 68 and representing an estimated eight hundred separate works.

The Dead Sea Scrolls comprise a vast collection of Jewish documents written in Hebrew, Aramaic, and Greek, and encompassing many subjects and literary styles. They include manuscripts or fragments of every book in the Hebrew Bible except the Book of Esther, all of them created nearly one thousand years earlier than any previously known biblical manuscripts. The scrolls also contain the earliest existing biblical commentary, on the Book of Habakkuk, and many other writings, among them religious works pertaining to Jewish sects of the time.

The Controversy Begins

The shepherd who made the discovery at Qumran brought the seven intact scrolls he found there to an antique dealer. Three were sold to a scholar at Hebrew University and four were sold to the Archbishop of Syria, who tried for years to place them with a reputable academic institution and ultimately sold them in 1954 through a classified ad in The Wall Street Journal. The ad was answered by Israeli archaeologist Yigael Yadin, who donated these scrolls to the state of Israel and established a museum for them, The Shrine of the Book, at Hebrew University.

*Control of the remaining tens of thousands of scroll fragments, however, was not soon resolved. One year after the discovery at Qumran, the United Nations partitioned Palestine and war began. Meanwhile, a U.N. -appointed, **Jesuit-trained** official had summoned Roland de Vaux, director of the Ecole Biblique, a French Catholic Theological School in Arab East Jerusalem, to oversee research on the scrolls. The slow pace of publication and the extreme secrecy of de Vaux's almost entirely Catholic group fueled the theory that the Vatican wished to suppress information in the scrolls."*

Countries eligible to sit on the UN Security Council:

Afghanistan, Albania, Algeria, Andorra, Angola, Antigua and Barbuda, Argentina, Armenia, Australia, Austria, Azerbaijan, Bahamas, Bahrain, Bangladesh, Barbados, Belarus, Belgium, Belize, Benin, Bhutan, Bolivia, Bosnia and Herzegovina, Botswana, Brazil, Brunei Darussalam, Bulgaria, Burkina Faso, Burundi, Cambodia, Cameroon, Canada, Cape Verde, Central African Republic, Chad, Chile, China, Colombia, Comoro Islands, Congo, Costa Rica, Cote d'Ivoire, Croatia, Cuba, Cyprus, Czech Republic, Democratic People's Republic of Korea, Democratic Republic of the Congo, Denmark, Djibouti, Dominica, Dominican Republic, Ecuador, Egypt, El Salvador, Equatorial Guinea, Eritrea, Estonia, Ethiopia, Fiji, Finland, France, Gabon, Gambia, Georgia, Germany, Ghana, Greece, Grenada, Guatemala, Guinea, Guinea-Bissau, Guyana, Haiti, Honduras, Hungary, Iceland, India, Indonesia, Iran, Iraq, Ireland, Italy, Jamaica, Japan, Jordan, Kazakhstan, Kenya, Kiribati, Kuwait, Kyrgyzstan, Laos, Latvia, Lebanon, Lesotho, Liberia, Libya, Liechtenstein, Lithuania, Luxembourg, Madagascar, Malawi, Malaysia, Maldives, Mali, Malta, Marshall Islands, Mauritania, Mauritius, Mexico, Micronesia, Moldova, Monaco, Mongolia, Morocco, Mozambique, Myanmar, Namibia, Nauru, Nepal, Netherlands, New Zealand, Nicaragua, Niger, Nigeria, Norway, Oman, Pakistan, Palau, Panama, Papua New Guinea, Paraguay, Peru, Philippines, Poland, Portugal, Qatar, Republic of Korea, Romania, Russian Federation, Rwanda, St. Kitts and Nevis, St. Lucia, St. Vincent and the Grenadines, Samoa, San Marino, Sao Tome and Principe, Saudi Arabia, Senegal, Seychelles, Sierra Leone, Singapore, Slovakia, Slovenia, Solomon Islands, Somalia, South Africa, Spain, Sri Lanka, Sudan, Suriname, Swaziland, Sweden, Syria, Tajikistan, Tanzania, Thailand, The Former Yugoslav Republic of Macedonia, Togo, Tonga, Trinidad and Tobago, Tunisia, Turkey, Turkmenistan, Uganda, Ukraine, United Arab Emirates, United Kingdom, United States, Uruguay, Uzbekistan, Vanuatu, Venezuela, Viet Nam, Yemen, Yugoslavia, Zambia, Zimbabwe.

Countries not eligible to sit on the UN Security Council: Israel

The Illuminati seeds to destroy civilization, so they may set those they choose in rulership. They openly serve ha shatan under a Latin term, "Lucifer", meaning "bringer of light". They infiltrate governments and businesses to set powers against one another.

All Illuminati members are 33rd Degree Masons.
The Illuminati strives to accomplish these main objectives:

1) Abolition of the Monarchy and all ordered government.
2) Abolition of private property.
3) Abolition of inheritance.
4) Abolition of patriotism.
5) Abolition of the family, through the abolition of marriage, all morality, and the institution of communal education for children.
6) Abolition of all religion.

THE MESSAGE OF THE GEORGIA GUIDESTONES:

1. Maintain humanity under 500,000,000 in perpetual balance with nature.
2. Guide reproduction wisely - improving fitness and diversity.
3. Unite humanity with a living new language.
4. Rule passion - faith - tradition - and all things with tempered reason.
5. Protect people and nations with fair laws and just courts.
6. Let all nations rule internally resolving external disputes in a world court.
7. Avoid petty laws and useless officials.
8. Balance personal rights with social duties.
9. Prize truth - beauty - love - seeking harmony with the infinite.
10. Be not a cancer on the earth - Leave room for nature - Leave room for nature.

The Knights Templar would be so proud to see how their

secret society influenced so many "modern" minds. They may have been upset about the red fez, but who cares. The red fez is another interesting study in itself, but we won't deal with it here. The evil won't succeed; Yahushua is going to surprise them at the moment they take over. Their "anti-Messiah", titled "Maitreya", will be slain by the brightness of Yahushua's coming. Maitreya's minions will also perish.

There will be 2 "denominations" in the world-to-come. One of them (Israel) will be permitted to enter the gates, and the other will have to remain outside:

ISRAEL (Rev. 21:12) ~ and ~ **DOGS** (Rev. 22:15)

That's all there is now; so the choice will be easy for us.
"No Dogs Allowed" signs might even be posted.

U.N.: Presently, probably the most dangerous organization on the face of the Earth. As time goes on, its fascist tentacles grow stronger and longer on the throat of this world. It is the instrument of the men who worship "reason", the illuminati. Watch the office of the Secretary General; but perceive the puppet masters behind the office - the elite globalists of the **N.W.O.**
Evolution/Darwinism,   Socialism/Communism,   Globalism/World Government, Atheism/Humanism; the public education of our children with these principles is their strategy. **The United Nations is a Humanist organization**, and will never give up.   Our knowledge of their agenda is the key to our freedom.   Those who know the **truth** cannot be controlled by evil and deception; **it sets us free.**   We can count on being persecuted for the Truth. Indeed, this is not new. If we were not persecuted, we would have to assume we were outside Yahuah's will.   For the most part, the unbelievers will tend to leave us alone. But the lies which are taught by the religious will be threatened when the Truth is revealed through the action of Yahushua's Spirit, through His people. We will experience confrontations with the religious "leadership" (human-appointed), indicating that they have spiritual strongholds that are causing them to be fearful of the Truth. We are **living swords** to them, so they are afraid for good reason.
This reminds me of Acts 5:27-32:

"Having brought the apostles, they made them appear

*before the Sanhedrin to be questioned by the high priest.
'We gave you strict orders not to teach in this name,' he
said. 'Yet you have filled Jerusalem with your teaching
and are determined to make us guilty of this man's
blood.' Kepha and the other apostles replied: 'We must
obey* [Elohim] *rather than men! The* [Elohim] *of our fathers
raised [Yahushua] from the dead - whom you had killed
by hanging Him on a tree. [Elohim] exalted Him to His
own right hand as Prince and Savior that He might give
repentance and forgiveness of sins to Israel. We are witnesses of these things, and so is the* [Ruach ha'Qodesh],
whom [Elohim] *has given to those who obey Him."*

We walk as lions among the meek and fearful who reject
the religion of Yahuah: the **Torah of Yahuah**.
And, it (Torah) has taught us the highest of all things there are
to learn: **LOVE.**

A Strong Delusion

You may have been programmed to believe error.

For many centuries, Christians have "believed" specific
things to be facts, yet their belief in some of them is un-
founded by Scripture.   Reality can be masked, or
"**misdirected**", by the skilled *suggestion* of magicians, hypno-
tists, and other types of deceivers. The "power of suggestion"
and the "placebo effect" were both popularized by the research of *Dr. Franz Anton Mesmer* (1734-1815).   Dr. Mesmer
studied the power of suggestion; he didn't discover it - it's
been around since the Fall of mankind. Hypnosis was developed from his research on psychological suggestion. When
people are exposed to errors *mixed* together with the truth,
they can become "mesmerized", moving the line between
what is real and what is not real in their belief system based
upon opinions - subtly suggested/taught by trusted "teachers"
they have made themselves subordinate to. To **misdirect** is
to *delude*. Certain **beliefs** are the direct result of the power of
suggestion. We can be naturally fascinated by a teacher,
and develop the response of aligning our beliefs to his repeated suggestions. The deceived deceivers bring up specific passages of Scripture, then "misdirect" (divert) your
thought process to make you think of something other than

what the text is actually saying. This is one example of "mesmerization". Notice the diversion tactic often used from the text of Acts 20. "They" want you to notice one thing; the phrase **"first day of the week"**, then hope you go numb to following the rest of the chapter. Acts 20:7-38 begins by describing a "gathering" of believers (Natsarim) in a home, an upper room, where they listened to Paul (Shaul) until midnight, since Paul was departing the following morning (which would still be the "first day" of the week). This was at Troas, where they had arrived after **"the days of unleavened bread"** (7 days following Passover). Have you been taught about "Unleavened Bread" or "Passover" as being a part of your annual observances? Also, notice **"there were many lamps in the upper room"** - this is mentioned by Luke because it was after dark. At the start of this gathering in the lamp-filled upper room, Sabbath had just ended, and a few of the Natsarim had come together in this private home, and had a bite together (breaking bread). It was after sunset, the resting was over. It was officially the "first day of the week" when Sabbath ended at sunset. There was nothing going on here like a "Mass", or a "communion service". In fact, no one was "worshipping". The believers simply wanted to hear Paul (Shaul) before he left town. Next, they sailed on to Miletos, and called the *ELDERS* of Ephesos there, to hear an important matter. This whole section needs to be carefully studied, because *WHAT SHAUL TAUGHT* them is over-looked because of the **distraction** to make you **think** about how it was "the first day of the week", stated earlier in the chapter. Get past that, study this chapter closely, and READ THE WARNING Shaul gave to the elders he had called for. It will shake you to your roots, and probably wake-up many of you from a life-long slumber. You should be able to see the "diversion tactic" that has been used to **block** the thoughts of people from seeing what Shaul wanted to warn us of.

Another diversion tactic is used at 2 Pet. 3:14-18. They try to make you **think** about Shaul's letters being *"Scriptures"*, to *distract you* from what is being said -- it's another warning to us. Our main job is to overcome the errors, so we can be effective in our service and reach the LOST with the Truth, the Word, the Torah of the Maker of Heaven and Earth. Our message to them is "Repent, for the reign of YHWH draws near." Repentance means return to the Torah (Ten Words, the Covenant) -- but it has been turned into a misunderstanding, where "grace" and "being under law" are considered to be in conflict with each other. To partake of the New Covenant (Jer. 31, Heb. 8), we must *receive a love for the Torah*, allowing Yahushua to circumcise our hearts with a love for it.

"Therefore, go and make taught ones of all the nations, immersing them into the Name of the Father and of the Son and of the Set-apart Spirit, teaching them to guard all that I have commanded you." Mt. 28:19. *How much* of what He had commanded were they to teach "all the nations"? Answer: ". . . all that I have commanded you." Surely, the 10 Commandments are involved in *"all that I have commanded you"* -- don't you imagine? This is the work we must <u>all</u> do, not just the "leaders" of our assemblies. Really, Yahushua is the only "leader" we have, and "pastors" are simply organizers. And not all pastors do things in the same way, nor is all pastoring the same. There are a variety of functions and members in Yahushua's Body, His living Temple. Our ministry (work) is different from most others, but no more or less vital to the health of the overall Body.

The answer to the delusion is in Genesis, or what is called "Bereshith" in the original Hebrew, all the way through to Revelation; that we are to rest from all our work as YHWH did on the seventh day of every week. It's given clearly as a directive in the book of Exodus, the 4th of the Ten Commandments. The Sabbath is spoken of 9 times in the book of Acts. It is called "a sign" (oth) between YHWH and Israel, the only sign of the "everlasting Covenant" (Ex. 31:13-17, Ez. 20:12-20, directly referred to at Heb. 4). At Hebrews 4, we are told specifically that the "rest" involves the 7th day of the week, and that for the "people of Elohim" there remains a Sabbath-keeping. How could they get around that? Simple; by misdirecting the meaning, and deluding the listeners. They have even "suggested" picking a day out of every 7 to rest -- but when you pick the correct one, you're "legalistic". Well, that's better than being "illegalistic" I'd say. If the Covenant is everlasting, its sign is also: the weekly Sabbath. Our Messiah, Rabbi Yahushua, made the heavens and the Earth, and called them as witnesses to this Covenant, and as long as they endure, the Ten Commandments will stand, not just 9 of them. Not one letter can be altered. The Sabbath He kept is not the one Christianity recognizes, simply because Christianity is a religion ABOUT Him, and is not the same religion He teaches and adheres to Himself. Constantine changed the day of rest to his "SUN-day". Setting aside the Commandments of YHWH in order to adhere to human traditions is very dangerous, as is worship in a way that is humanly invented. You must think outside of the box to get past some strong deceptions. Many deceptive ideas and customs have been "hidden" in plain sight, openly practiced for all to see. Yet all the while those who promote these ideas have to constantly provide an explanation for them, like a "booster shot", to keep the masses under the spell of their "vaccination" against the real truth. Being under the spell of their excuses makes the listener "drunk", and numb to the truth when it does come along. The fact is, those who are "deluded" don't know they are. If they knew, they would not allow the delusion to continue. The truth comes with a price tag: giving up the comfort of feeling secure in one's beliefs about reality at any cost in order to attain the truth. It means we have to be prepared to "wake up" and become aware of our previous and/or existing delusions. The movie Matrix comes to mind immediately, since it portrays these circumstances clearly. Some of us are completely "awake", but walking around in a world with the majority of people "dreaming" a reality that's not really there at all. We want to share the truth with you, but you don't even realize that you're "dreaming" or living in a constructed matrix someone designed for you to remain deluded in.2 Thess 2:7-12 is critical to understand that there is delusion, the working of error:

"7 For the mystery of lawlessness (the secret of "Torahlessness", living without law) is already at work; only he who now restrains (controls) will do so until he is taken out of the way. 8 And then the lawless one will be revealed, whom the Master will consume with the breath of His mouth and destroy with the brightness of His coming. 9 The coming of the lawless one is according to the working of Satan, with all power, signs, and lying wonders, 10 and with all unrighteous deception among those who perish, because they did not receive the love of the truth, that they might be saved. 11 And for this reason (Elohim) will send them strong delusion, that they should believe the lie, 12 that they all may be condemned who did not believe the truth but had pleasure in un-righteousness." The word "delusion" used here is translated from the Greek word, PLANOS, #4106 — and means a wrong opinion, errors in morals, a leading astray, a working of error. How can we tell if we are under a spell or hypnotic trance? Is it possible to test for such a condition in ourselves? The only sure test to find out if we are deluded is to do a personal topical study of Scripture, and compare what we learn from this study with our "reality" as we have perceived it to be. We must be careful to let Scripture speak alone, without our bringing any former beliefs to the study we are undertaking. This will be very sobering to everyone who takes time to test themselves in this way. If you are like 99% of sincere Christians, you honestly believe that "Sun-Day" is the "Christian Sabbath". At the same time, you may have been told that "Jewish" believers in the same Messiah may observe the usual "7th day" of the week Sabbath, because they were "BORN" as Jewish-folk. So, we immediately have re-built a dividing wall that had been removed by Messiah's death and resurrection (Eph. 2:14). Instead of ONE body, we have TWO bodies of Messiah, based on the distinction of being BORN as a Jewish person, or as a Gentile person. This surely cannot be -- it turns out to only be one of many "human traditions", brought about by a working of error (a delusion!). As you slowly read the book of Acts, you will discover the truth of the matter - never has the 4th Commandment (the Sabbath) been "changed" by any doctrine originating in Scripture. The first chapter of Acts will reveal this to you. A delusion (working of error) has hypnotically entranced most of the world in a deception practiced openly. Oh, but there's much, much more to be revealed. Are you prepared to fully awaken? The next level will cause you great pain, yet you will be so grateful for reaching it. You will meet with your pastor after you awaken, and he will show you a side of himself you never knew to exist. He will seem to be "asleep" to you.Topics that you should personally study to test yourself for being deluded:

The Sabbath - has anyone changed which day is the Sabbath mentioned in the 10 Commandments? Sure they have - it was imposed by Roman emperor Constantine I. But can the change be found in Scripture? Well, yes; but it's a bad thing -- read Daniel 7:25. It may be that it is linked to the "mark of the beast" (Rev. 13) since "buying and selling" is NOT allowed to be done on the Sabbath Day. Those having the beast's mark (Sun-Day?) are allowed to buy and sell, but those having YHWH's mark (the Sabbath) are not permitted to buy and sell -- but this is self imposed on these obedient folks, only pertaining to the day of rest. Scripture refers to those who disobey the Covenant (Torah) as dogs and beasts. The Commandments -- and those obedient to them out of love -- reveal who is of YHWH and who is a servant of the deceiver of this world. (And this article is about delusion, deception, and error).

The Personal Name of our Creator - has it been intentionally concealed and removed from the common translations, according to their own admission in the preface? Have you ever looked up the word "GOD" in a good encyclopedia to learn the origins of the word?

Messiah's real Name - Is there only one (Acts 4:12), and is it Yahushua or Jesus?

The re-newed, or "New Covenant" - What is it? Can we find it in the Scriptures? (see Jer. 31, Ez. 36, Heb. 8).

Bible - is this word found in the Scriptures, or ever used by Scripture to refer to itself? Or, is it a Pagan deity's name? (investigate Biblia, Biblos). To wet your appetite for more, here's a glimpse at some TRUTH:

This is what the Encyclopedia Americana (1945 Edition) says under the topic "GOD":"GOD (god): Common Teutonic word for personal object of religious worship, formerly applicable to super-human beings of heathen myth; on conversion of Teutonic races to Christianity, term was applied to Supreme Being." NO! IT CAN'T BE TRUE! But it is true. Rabbi Yahushua haMashiach informed us that the Scriptures bear witness of Him (Jn. 5:39). He also told us He is the Master of the Sabbath (Mk 2:28), and to pray that our flight not be in winter or on a Sabbath (Mt. 24:20 - an END TIME warning). It is the sign of the everlasting Covenant (Ex. 31, Ez. 20), yet following human misdirection, we are easily deluded to believe it has been changed to Sun-Day. Human reasoning hypnotically explains our reality for us, while Scripture is completely silent about any change in Sabbath observance. Paul (or Shaul), the same fellow that most people quote to explain how they don't have to obey the Covenant (Torah), told us to "TEST" ourselves to see if we are in the true faith (2Cor.

13:5). I would ask no more of any of you. If YHWH is going to severely punish the nations that fail to observe the feast of Booths (Sukkoth) during the Millennial Reign (Zech. 14), how much will He punish those who completely ignore ALL His Sabbaths? Another question to ask yourself is, would He punish anyone who stepped out of the line of "lemmings" and actually obeyed Him by resting on the 7th day of every week? Only the other lemmings are going to get upset over it. When sent to "basic training", young men are re-programmed to suppress their moral character, and to obey orders to KILL on demand. This "brain-washing" doesn't work on each individual, however the goal is to have enough affected that the objective is still achieved. When the principles of psychological suggestion are applied to religious control, the same effect is achieved -- repeated suggestions to suppress moral character (the conscience that warns us of being out-of-bounds) will brain-wash most of those exposed to it.

I DARE YOU!

The following tract is intended to challenge Christians of **all** denominations to think carefully about what some human traditions may look like in the Eyes of our Creator. In the world-to-come, when we are resurrected and clothed with immortality, there will be TWO "denominations".
Which denomination is Yahushua of?

Please consider taking a dare. This is a challenge for you to think outside of "the box", your denomination.
(You'll thank me later).
Which "denomination" is the right one? In the world-to-come, there will be "two" denominations. Read this article, and you'll find out what they are. A basic struggle we all have is getting at the Truth, and seeing things from our Creator's point-of-view. We all have *beliefs*, but what we really need is the Truth; the true *facts*. We have to stop limiting things to man's point-of-view alone.

At Deut. 12:30-32, we are commanded to not learn the "ways" of the Pagans (to not learn or adopt formats or traditions which Pagans used to serve their idols), nor worship YHWH in **their** way. That eliminates the excuse that is most popular: that because **we** aren't thinking about worshipping YHWH in a Pagan way, then the previous Pagan activity is

PAGAN: LATIN, "RURAL-DWELLER". LATER, BECAME TERM FOR HEATHEN

"cleansed" of all its pagan origins and intentions. If _intentions_ are what makes things OK, YHWH would have told us this; but the golden calf was made with the _intention_ of worshipping YHWH, and we see that the whole nation of Israel was almost destroyed. "Pagan" is the same thing as "Satanic". Sorcery, astrology, or magic (black or white) are all the "works of the devil". Worshipping YHWH in a way He did not develop is very dangerous. Most of you are aware that "Halloween" is a previously Pagan observance, and have begun by withdrawing your family's involvement in it - and you've felt the heat from family and friends over it too. Well, you need to look carefully into the origins of the holidays we've inherited called "Christmas" and "Easter" as well. Relax, because the Truth and your belief in our Messiah and His Word will stand firm; but you will discover that "Christmas" and "Easter" are no different than Halloween - formerly they were Pagan observances which became camouflaged and revised to appear as something different than they really are. Paganism, witchcraft, and Satanism are all the same thing -- rebellion against YHWH. You will hear all sorts of excuses for theses holidays, and the heat you've felt over Halloween is nothing compared to what you will be feeling when you learn the true background of Christmas and Easter. The very religious Pilgrims that came to the continent of North America in the 15th century were fleeing severe persecution for their understandings of Scripture, and the first colonies established had laws on the books which outlawed the Pagan observance of Christmas -- because they all knew what it really was. This all became more relaxed as increasing numbers of Irish Catholics immigrated to this continent. The Colonials didn't like the Irish very much, because of their Catholicism -- the thing many of them had fled from. It wasn't because they were Irish! The idea of "SUN-DAY" being the Sabbath, changed during the 4th century, is another area that generates a lot of heat.

If you need a Christmas tree, or a chocolate bunny rabbit & Easter eggs, or wish to change the day of rest which YHWH has established, and you don't know there's anything wrong, then you are without a knowledge of sin (Jn. 15:22). 1 Cor. 9:21 should be a strong warning for those "without the law" however. When you have been told, and investigate what

Scripture says about these things, and don't repent, you are responsible; and guilty of an even greater transgression. These pagan traditions are idolatry, because they originated in idolatry. The RCC used "missionary adaptation" on us, inculturating formerly Pagan elements in populations to "convert" the people using their familiar patterns of worship. In other words, the Pagan format remained intact, but the meaning of the terms, symbols, and traditions were altered; and Scripture had to be suppressed to pull it off.

In the Creator's eyes, these Pagan elements cannot be washed and changed into anything else. A pig, after it is cleaned up, is still a pig, even if you put lipstick on it and pretend it's changed. Converts who have been cleaned from their idolatry are like pigs if their hearts are not converted. But, the Jesuits and Dominicans don't care about YHWH; the "end" justifies the "means". Like pigs, they too will return to their mud hole, and like a dog, return to their vomit. The lure is just too much.

The context of Romans 14 is speaking about "special days", because the Yahudim had human traditions concerning fasting twice each week. If someone didn't follow the pattern, they were regarded as less pious. Shaul (Paul) was simply declaring that what we do or don't do is OK, fasting or not, but he is not condoning the adoption of previously pagan customs and traditions to honor YHWH with them. This is going far beyond the intention of what Shaul wrote. Shaul is commonly misunderstood to be sure. Peter warned us not to misunderstand Shaul's writings.

Often, it is said, "Christians do not have to observe any particular day". Most have been taught that SUN-DAY is the "Christian Sabbath", and even believing this they will buy and sell or work on this day, the 1st day of each week. They will agree, however, that their SUN-DAY is certainly not the Sabbath that Yahushua observed.

HOW MUST WE LIVE?

How we live is a mixture of how we were molded and taught, and what we have chosen to accept or reject. Our walk reveals who we really serve, even if we are deceived about who that is. The Hebraic concept of how we live is called "halakah", from the word halak, referring to our "walk". The "way" or "path" on which we do this "walking" is either the

narrow path of light (as Torah directs us in its teachings/
directions), or the broad road of darkness that follows no directions from Torah. This road of darkness without Torah
leads to death (the eternal kind). The Torah is the way, our
map, to direct us into "paths of righteousness" which YHWH
guides us into "for His Name's sake". All who call on His true
Name must depart from all unrighteousness, or it brings
shame upon His Name. Yahushua is "the way", the living
Torah (Word of YHWH), and the light. His religion -- the way
He lives -- is the only way; there's no other way to enter
eternal life but through the gateway. You cannot invent your
own way, or path, and sneak in without accepting the love for
the Truth, which is His Torah. He will give you this love for
His Torah, but you have to want it, and ask Him for it. How
do you live? Most of us are raised in a denomination or
mold, called "a religion". These may be about the Messiah,
but are any of them the Messiah's religion? 1 Yn 2:6
says,"The one who says he stays in Him ought himself also to
walk, even as He walked." Do we need to have a degree in
Theology to understand what that sentence might mean?
Further, 2 Yn. 1:6 tells us,

"And this is the love, that we walk according to His Commands. This is the Command, that as you have heard from
the beginning, you should walk in it." Our obedience is the
evidence of our faithfulness, and shows YHWH that we are
His servants, and we're not inventing our own methodology or
following any humanly-designed process. The Commandments are not new, and neither can they be revoked; they
define what a sin is (see 1 Yn. 3:4, Jas. 1:22-25). The New
(or renewed) Covenant is having these Commands written
upon our hearts and minds by Yahushua's Spirit (Heb. 8).
Even SATAN is a believer (Ya'aqob/James 2:19) . . . but this
rebellious being will not serve and obey!

It's how we walk (our halakah) that reveals the truth about
whether our "religion" is His religion, or is just about Him.
One path is the path of light, guided by the Torah, and the
other is designed by traditions of men to win the approval of
men — seminary-trained, but flawed in their walk, having exchanged the Commandments of YHWH for the traditions of
men. Unless your conscience is completely numbed by listening to the intoxicating excuses and deceiving teachings,

you know that most have fulfilled the prophecy that there would be an "apostasy", or falling-away from the Torah, the true faith. It can only be determined by what is right, or right-eous, as defined by the Torah — not the masquerading messengers of light who fill our heads with traditional lies that have no basis from Scripture. Test everything, especially the excuses you are taught, and ask for the clear Scriptural foundation they base their teachings upon. If we are taught that we no longer have to obey a Commandment, there had better be clear Scriptural verses to show this to be true. A good place to start investigating would be to study the 4th Commandment, concerning the "Shabbath", which commands us to rest on the 7th day of each week — in commemoration of Creation week. Has this Commandment been annulled by YHWH, or men? Can men alter any of the Commandments? They may claim they have the authority, but Scripturally this is simply not true. Catholics have claimed the authority to "bind and loose" is in the hands of men, however these words simply mean "forbid and permit", and the men (elders) who can do this are intended to be guided solely by a thorough knowledge of Torah (what YHWH has spoken in His Word). Men have departed from the Torah, and the "apostasy" is this falling away from Torah. "Nicolaitans" have invented their own way of serving, and it's been designed to make them rich - borrowing heavily from Pagan backgrounds. Consequently, we see many things "forbidden and permitted" which are simply the whims of men, apart from the counsel of Scripture. They tickle people's ears to make things feel warm and fuzzy for everyone. The conscience which YHWH put within us is supposed to warn us when we do wrong, but if it is "seared", or short-circuited with false doctrine, it cannot do this. When we drink clean water (Truth) and poisoned water (false doctrine) together, it is what Scripture calls "wormwood", and we are in a stupor. Most people stay "drunk" on this wormwood, flowing from pulpits each week. Words of men tickle their ears, and they are constantly made to feel at ease, but they remain in idolatrous sin.

Our "worship" is really obedience, the doing of what YHWH expects of us. If we neglect doing what He expects of us, but assume our intentions will serve the same results, then we didn't understand the Fall, the golden calf incident, nor why Qayin's (Cain's) offering was not pleasing to YHWH. "If you do well, shall you not be accepted?" (Gen. 4:7). Qayin made up his own mind how he was going to worship YHWH, and what would be the offering. How is Christianity any different? All the Sun-day assemblies, Christmas trees, and Easter baskets in the world will not be acceptable to YHWH, unless He prescribed them as a form of worshipping Him. So, our simple task is to find out what YHWH expects, then "do well" so that He will accept our worship of Him. Then, we can expect to hear the words, "Well done , good and faithful servant!" (Mt. 25:21). Doing "the Word" is obeying Him, not adding to it, or taking away from it, or adopting the Pagan cultural background as tradition has done.

Read Acts, and circle the word Sabbath each time it is used. What was Dr. Luke mentioning the "Sabbath" for? Many say, "We aren't Jewish, so we don't have to obey the 4th Commandment". Well, why stop there? Why not say, "We aren't Jewish, so we don't have to worry about the 7th and 8th Commandment". ~ What?
Here's where the rubber meets the road - What is the New (or re-newed) Covenant? If it is something different, please tell me:

The New Covenant

(See Jeremiah 31, Hebrews 8, Hebrews 10)
Here's what it is: Yahushua ha'Mashiach *writes* His Torah (teachings, Commandments) on our hearts. We *receive a love for the Truth*, His **Word**, which is the **Covenant**, or Ten Words. It's as simple as that. This process involves being convicted of sin (by learning the Commandments), repenting (stop sinning, turn back to them), and being immersed into His Name. This immersion is the outward sign of the "circumcision" of our heart, by the Spirit of the Mashiach, Who lives in us from that point on. I cannot convince you or convict you of your sin (rebellion against YHWH's Covenant, the Ten Commandments) -- but Yahushua can change your heart, which is your only hope. The mind of the flesh cannot, and will not, obey. I love YHWH's Ten Commandments. Would you like to love them too?

I dare you -- say, "I want to love the Commandments too." Yahushua's Spirit is all around you, and He WILL grab you if you return to His Covenant. This is what happened to the prodigal son, the moment he took his first step out of the pig pen, to return to His Father's house, the Torah/Covenant. Take that step -- ask Him to write His Torah on your heart. He has promised to do this if you will repent, believing on His Name.

If I were a servant of the adversary, would I promote the obedience to the Covenant made between Israel (YHWH's wife) and the Creator, YHWH? You may have never heard it before, but you must engraft into Israel to partake of the Covenant(s) (see Romans 11). You do not "replace" Israel, you engraft into the olive tree. You may likely be of a "wild" olive tree, a foreigner to the cultivated garden of YHWH, Israel. The "sign" of the everlasting Covenant is the sign of the Sabbath Day, which rolls around each week. My legal proof is Ex. 31:13-17, quoted again at Hebrews 4:4-11. Without this sign, can you be in a Covenant of any kind with YHWH, based on what Scripture teaches? Is. 48:10 speaks of an iron furnace, a furnace of affliction, an unfriendly environment which refines and tests us constantly. Many of us are in that furnace now, being tested who we will serve. As for me and my house, we will serve YHWH. We are the servant of the one whom we obey. Look at the 12 gates into the New Jerusalem (Rev. 21:12-15) -- each one is named for a tribe of Israel. There's no Christian gate, no Islamic gate, no Hindu gate. Welcome to all those who join Israel, and observe the Commandments of YHWH. If you want to really scare yourself, ignore everything I've told you. If you want more proof, read Isaiah 56. Actually, read chapters 55, 56, and 57.

Consider the possibility that you may be intoxicated on wormwood, but you don't know it -- so study on your own, without the excuses ringing in your ears. You will find the Truth of every matter under Heaven. It may sound odd to put it this way, but "drinking" the intoxicating "wine" (doctrines) of misguided preachers will keep you numb — as if you are drunk — and you simply need to sober-up and do some personal research in the Scriptures. The excuses are "an eye of darkness", which seeks after ways of getting around the Commandments. An "eye filled with light" is that approach which pants after YHWH's Commandments, looking for more to learn so they can be obeyed. Which approach would Satan want you to take?   Remember, Satan is a believer too; but not an obeyor.   And if you obey, would that upset Yahushua, or the men and their traditions of setting aside the Commandments of YHWH?   You know the answer -- and if you act in the Truth, you'll be in the iron furnace with the rest of us.   Try obeying the Sabbath, and feel the heat we feel for it.   Walk like Yahushua. *I dare you.*

Concerning TRUTH:

I'm impressed with the way it was put by the 12th century Jewish "Rambam", Maimonides. He wrote:

"Men like the opinions to which they have been accustomed from their youth; they defend them, and shun contrary views; and this is one of the things that prevents men from finding truth, for they cling to the opinion of habit."

- Maimonides - Guide For The Perplexed

I found this at the Jewish Virtual Library:

Maimonides/Rambam: (1135-1204)

Maimonides's full name was Moses ben Maimon; in Hebrew he is known by the acronym of Rabbi Moses ben Maimon, Rambam. He was born in Spain shortly before the fanatical Muslim Almohades came to power there.   To avoid persecution by the Muslim sect — which was wont to offer Jews and Christians the choice of conversion to Islam or death — Maimonides fled with his family, first to Morocco, later to Israel, and finally to Egypt.

A translation improvement:

Here's something to consider that helps reduce the lawless interpretation people derive from Shaul's writing:

"In that He says, "A new covenant," He has made the first obsolete. Now what is becoming obsolete and growing old is ready to vanish away."

Ibrim (Hebrews) 8:13

This passage above using the word "covenant" has been commonly mistranslated - the **Greek** from which it is translated clearly shows the word "covenant" *is not present*, and the Greek language assumes the subject to be the topic being discussed.   The context demands that the word be **"priesthood",** since the change in **priesthood** is what is being discussed.   The KJV puts the word in *italics* as **covenant**, because it was added by the translators.   What was vanish-

155

Sophist in full costume

A
*"wise guy"
ready for
the
parade!*

"FRERE MACON"
(freemason)
meaning
brother mason

Greek deity
"Hermes"

ing away was the <u>priesthood</u>, with its sacrifices.   In fact, YHWH literally made the Temple vanish too.   This text needs to read:

"In that He says, "A new priesthood," He has made the first obsolete. Now what is becoming obsolete and growing old is ready to vanish away." Ibrim (Hebrews) 8:13

Kipa — (Dome) *also known as yarmulke*

In the Hebrew language, the word "Kippah" means **dome**. You may find it hard to believe, but the domed beanie-hat seen on popes, cardinals, orthodox rabbis, and some oriental folks is derived from the Greek hat of Hermes, the Greek deity of the mind. It is in fact the hat of Hermes. *Commerce, fortune, gymnastics, cunning, and shrewdness* were celebrated in his honor. Hermes is really big with the Masons. To them he's the "god" of wisdom, also known as Thoth or Set. You've seen adaptations of his hat worn by graduates and their professors, but slightly disguised beneath a square "mortar board", another weird custom inherited from the guilds (sort of union-run schools) of the Middle Ages.   Ceremonies and "initiations" are very important to the hood-winkery that they engage in. Take a gander at the happy fellow pictured wearing the robes of a scholar. The Latin word "doctor" means *teacher.*

They taught building techniques and architecture, and were students of "masonry" -- which relates to the "mortar board" hat over the domed beanie. The guys in guilds who built the buildings were REAL masons (stonemasons), not members of the Blue Lodge, fiddling with swords and dreaming of being secret knights. When these brutes put on *their* "aprons of righteousness" with all the little symbols on them, it meant they had paid their union dues -- so they could work "righteously" (in good standing), and not working without being a guild member in good standing. When you research the origin of a little hat called a "FEZ", you'll see it's linked to all this information. 33rd degree Masons (the Adepts / Illuminati) are fond of wearing a big red FEZ with a tassel on it. This is just great fun, isn't it? Now when you watch them put on their "caps and gowns" at the graduation ceremonies, you can snicker under your breath a little, knowing they have NO CLUE why they are wearing such a costume. The following is a brief excerpt from the book, Fossilized Customs:

"Yarmulke" is a Yiddish word for the kipa, or skullcap seen worn by the pope, and most orthodox Yahudim on the street, in the classroom, and in the synagogues. Mosheh would not know what it is. Alfred J. Kolatch, an orthodox author and "rabbi", states: "The skullcap has no religious significance in Jewish law." He goes on to say that it has no basis in Scriptural or Rabbinical law. To trace the use of the cap to its source, we find that it came into wider use only in the 17th century, where before that only a very few Yahudim used it. Did Rabbi Yahushua wear a kipa? All researchers and historians say NO, and there is no evidence of its use in any data or archaeological finds at all. The pope of Rome and his car-

Sophists Sophists were 5th century BC Greek philosophers who specialized in providing instruction in ethics and the art of public speaking. They were skilled in swaying opinions by using plausible-sounding arguments, and using faulty reasoning to convince their listeners of elaborate perversions of the truth. They were highly respected, paid speakers, who dressed in robes of honor, like a graduate or choir person does today - that's where these garments came from. Expert devisers of subtle tricks in speaking, their cleverness was highly refined, urbane, and cultured. This "sophistry" has been put to use in training men for the ministry throughout the centuries.

Most of the "church fathers" were sophists.

dinals wear them, but that is because it was originally a Greek hat of a scholar, called the "hat of Hermes" (Hermes is a Pagan idol, of course). You will recall the "cap and gown" of graduates from schools and universities employs this "hat of Hermes", topped with a square mason's board. A mason is a layer of bricks, and the mason's board holds the cement mix. These were scholars who graduated to different levels in their guilds; from apprentice to journeyman, then journeyman to master. In ancient times, just prior to 186 BCE, the land of Yisrael was ruled by a Greek Seleucid, Antiochus Epiphanes IV. He was extremely cruel, and outlawed the Hebrew religion, forcing his Greek customs on them. In the record of 2 Maccabees, an apostate high priest (named "Jason" in translation, but really named Y'shua) helped this Greek ruler impose the Greek ways of living: *"And abrogating the lawful way of living, he introduced new customs contrary to the Torah; for he willingly established a gymnasium right under the citadel (the Temple), and he made the finest of the young men wear the Greek hat."* (Recall that Hermes, the Greek deity of the mind, was associated with skills in commerce, fortune, gymnastics, cunning, and shrewdness. Reading the previous quote carefully, it is obvious that the "gymnasium" and the "finest of the young men" are linked to the special "hat" they were made to wear. This strongly implies that Hermes was involved, and the prowess and skill of the young men was rewarded. The hat must have been an icon or badge of honor to the Greeks for skill in gymnastics, leaving no doubt that Hermes would be the deity related to the hat.) Paul writes at 1Cor. 11:7 that a man is not to have his head covered in the assembly, but a woman is required to, to keep from dishonoring one another's headship. Yahushua is the man's 'head', while a woman's 'head' is her husband. We are to follow the Torah, and not add to it in any way: *"Do not add to nor take away from it"*. Dt. 12:32. Man-made customs, including all the camouflaged Paganism found in Christendom, are traditions that are forbidden in the worship of YHWH. They represent more than a "strange fire", but are like the golden calf. It is forbidden to worship Him after the customs of the Pagans. *"The one who says he abides in Him ought himself to walk in the same manner as He walked."* ~ 1 Yoch. 2:6. Walk in Light ~ the Torah.

Here's *more* historical data on the use of the kipa (dome), the Greek hat of Hermes:

The kipa or yarmulke is discussed in several books I've read by Orthodox rabbis, and they agree it is of human invention. And, they admit it has been a tradition for many centuries, but only became "popularized" because many people began to wear them during the 17th and 18th centuries. "Monkey see, monkey do" and false piety (hypocrisy) drives many things of this nature, no doubt.

One book I managed to easily put my hands on tonight is "The Jewish Book Of Why", by Alfred J. Kolatch (possibly some data about him is on the internet). I also have the "Second Jewish Book Of Why" stored somewhere. On page 2 of the former book, our Jewish brother writes:

"Were a Jew of the generation of Moses or Solomon or Judah the Maccabee alive today,
(obviously he misuses the term "Jew" here, since Mosheh was of the tribe of Lewi)

he would be quite confused as he observed our religious conduct. He would look at the talit (prayershawl) or kipa (skullcap) that we wear and ask, 'Why do Jews wear them? What are they for?' He would notice the gartl (girdle) and shtreiml (fur hat) worn by the chassid and be puzzled by the special garb."

He goes on and on, listing many things that Mosheh and the others would not know anything about, nor understand. And Alfred writes from the perspective of an Orthodox Yahudi, explaining things "Jewish" to other "Jews" who wonder about them - there is little doubt we Natsarim would wonder also!

On page 121 of the book, "*The Jewish Book Of Why*", by Alfred J. Kolatch, he continues more on the subject of the yarmulke   *(My comments will be in parenthesis & italics):*

Why are yarmulkes worn?

"A yarmulke, called a kipa in Hebrew, is a skullcap worn by Jews. Some wear one at all times, others only during prayer and at mealtime. The earliest Jewish reference to a head-covering can be found in Exodus 28:4, where it is called a **mitznefet**. It was part of the wardrobe of the High Priest. In other biblical reference, the covering of the head and face is regarded as a sign of mourning (II Samuel 15:30). The Talmud, however, associates the wearing of a headgear more with the concept of reverence (to God) and respect (for men of stature)".   *(He's left the reality of Torah, and entered the "reasoning" of man's tradition, adding to the Torah).*

"The word yarmulke is Yiddish, but of uncertain meaning. One view is that the word is derived from the head-covering called **armucella**, worn by medieval clergy."   *(Oops, the Pagan stuff is starting to pop up; but let's see how he shrugs it off and hypnotizes himself and the readers).*

"A more probable explanation is that the word yarmulke is related to the French arme (akin to the Latin arma), a type of round medieval helmet with a movable visor."
(Ah, "more probable" because the "movable visor" similarity on traditional Jewish yarmulkes makes an obvious connection!).

"Another Yiddish word for yarmulke is koppel (kappel), a form of the Latin capitalis, meaning 'of the head'."
(Great . . . now we're explaining it using Latin. In reality, the Latin word "capitalis" describes the domed temple of Jupiter, the "head" and highest official building in the Roman Empire. "Kippah" still means DOME in Hebrew, but Alfred never brings that up at all).

"The more traditional view is that the word yarmulke is a distorted form of the Hebrew words yaray may Elohim, 'in fear (awe) of God.'   This idea is based, for the most part, on a statement made by a fifth-century Babylonian talmudic scholar, **Huna ben Joshua**, who said, 'I never walked four cubits with uncovered head because God dwells over my head' (Kiddushin 31a)." (*Well that's really special brother Huna! But, what are you trying to do, make up something you hope YHWH will really take a fancy to - that He didn't ask for? See, that's exactly what Aharon's sons did when they offered the "strange fire", and somewhat like when Cain offered veggies instead of the correct offering. We can't make up this stuff as we go along. If Mosheh had approached the burning bush without shoes on, do you imagine YHWH would have told him to either put on some shoes or cover his head? Mosheh took something OFF, he didn't put something on. In the natural world, we "take our hats off to" those we hold in esteem. If you walk into a building and don't remove your hat, you could be a redneck*).

ALFRED CONTINUES:

"The custom of covering the head received wide acceptance, but not by all. Historian Israel Abrahams points out that in the thirteenth century "boys in Germany and adults in France were called to the Tora in the synagogue bareheaded."

"In the Middle Ages, French and Spanish rabbinical authorities regarded the practice of covering the head during prayer and when studying Torah to be no more than mere custom. Some rabbis were known to pray bareheaded. Today, Orthodox Jews and many Conservative Jews believe that covering the head is an expression of yirat Shama'yim 'fear of God' or 'reverence for God'." (*kind of a bad rendering there - more literally "respect for heavens"*).

"Orthodoxy demands that the head be kept covered at all times, while most Conservative Jews believe the head should be covered during prayer. In most Reform congragations covering the head during prayer is optional."
(End of book quote).

Not **Torah**, but **Orthodoxy demands** that the head be covered at all times. Personally, I can't recall seeing a single relief or drawing on a jar of any ancient Israelite ever wearing anything on their heads (aside from Lewites dressed for their duties). Even if an image can be found, it doesn't signify anymore than wearing sunglasses does. But, if you want to "reason" back and forth between what men think, we can stay stuck on this one point endlessly. To find out the Truth, the only way to get there is to reason it out with YHWH's Word. But, you can't exactly do that and win the debate - it's not mentioned.

The DOME shape itself is derived from ancient Pagan symbolism, and was absorbed into the architecture of Christianity and Islam directly from Pagan temple architecture. The "eye" of the Sun (the principal Pagan deity) was able to "see" into his temple through an "oculus" at the upper-most section of the dome, which was simply an enormous hole in the top (see Pantheon, Rome). In some Christian "churches" (they often refer to a "church" as a building), the domed architecture will even include an enormous EYE centered in the center of the dome, looking down at the congregation. Creepy. One of the most famous DOMED structures in the world was the Roman temple called the Pantheon, dedicated to many Roman deities. The dome was a secret allusion to the "dome of the sky", which the Pagans worshipped profusely. The word "domus" is Latin for "house", the dwelling or temple of Pagan deities in this case - but it also gives us words like "domestic". Dome is also slang for "head". "Dominus" means "lord". The domed building called "St. Peter's Cathedral" is directly modeled after the former Roman temples, and many government buildings around the world designed and built by Masons sport the Pagan architecture proudly. If you really dig, you'll find the shape is entirely rooted in the old Pagan theme, sex - - just as the steeples and obelisks are. The ancient root, dem, means to "join together", as it relates to sex. Look at the word "con-dom", and you see it. The word dominam was

used for the male member. But keep reading . . .

The wearing of "special" garments came directly from the Roman magisterial system, along with the philosophical idea that "the clothes make the man". Hierarchical positions of authority were mimicked from the Roman system of government. The nicolaitan approach to the functions within Yahushua's Body quickly became the norm, and Yahushua's authority was usurped by men, ranking their positions over one another.

The early "church fathers" were **former Pagans**, and were also teachers who regularly spoke before large audiences. The term for their important position was "**Sophist**" (from the Greek for *wise, clever*), and they were essentially professional speakers.   The "3-point-speech" technique was refined by these hired speakers, who were among the most highly-honored people of their day.   The practice of eating a dinner and listening to a renowned speaker comes to us from the Greek culture. They wore a distinctive costume, similar to the robes of a court judge today. They would also drape their robes with any ribbons or awards they may have received in the past, to punctuate their importance.
Have another quick look at the "wise guy" on page 155.

Whenever we want to know about something that we may be a little confused about, all we have to do is picture Yahushua, and ask ourselves what His opinion might be. Knowing how humble He is, it's doubtful He would wear a special garment to make us notice Him.   When He was engaged in washing the feet of His students, they were debating who among them was the greatest -- they were already trying to decide their "rank".   The home assembly for Scripture study is the best arrangement, however you might want to leave the "special" garment idea out. The urge to wear such things is not coming from our humble Mashiach, but rather the world.   Yahushua had no form or splendor, nor appearance that we should desire Him. He was despised and rejected by men - He didn't dress to fit in. (see Yesha Yahu 53).

So, why would anyone want to feel special wearing a little domed hat, wearing a dome on their dome?   Obviously to make a statement. Hats were often used to designate a person's status.   They added the propellers much later on (beanie-copters), and "dunce hats" were very popular with the school kids of long ago. Roman priests used hats to announce their office in the Church. Santa Claus wears a "Phrygian hat", exactly like the Roman deity "Mithras". Pagan priests also shaved their heads in various ways; one way was called a "tonsure", where the entire crown of the head above the ears was shorn, displaying the mark of their slavery to the SUN. The caps may have provided some protection from the sun's burning rays on the sensitive exposed scalps. But, that's only a guess, since the origin of the tonsure itself is buried in antiquity - but it is suspected to have been linked in some way to sun worship. Some people will believe anything you tell them, and will imitate what others do without question. I've heard that if you wrap your head up in a towel that is colored purple, the aliens (from outer space) will not be able to read your mind. No doubt, there's someone living near Roswell, New Mexico, that believes this. UFO museums would have no customers at all if people weren't so easily misguided.

Many people have read the Scriptures, and it's a sure thing that this behavior isn't described in them. But, there are examples of people starting up their own "strange" patterns, like the worshipping of the golden calf, and the serpent on the pole. YHWH had them grind these two objects to powder, and *drink them*. Are you thinking what I'm thinking? Re-

These domes, walls, hats, and so forth are being shoved into YHWH's face continually. Have you ever heard the expression, "I'll eat my hat"? If you don't wear one, you won't have to eat it. But YHWH could still require some things to be ground to powder and eaten, as He required Israel to do with the golden calf, and the serpent on the pole.

search on the "tradition" of Jewish men wearing a hat, we find that Catholic communities in Medieval times found it difficult to identify who was Jewish and who was not. All were bare-headed. So, the Catholics required the Jewish men to wear

IT'S AN ENTIRE KIPA VILLAGE! WITHOUT THE COSTUMES, THEY COULDN'T PULL THIS OFF.

PAGAN MITRE FOR HIGH PRIEST OF JANUS

KIPAS, DOMES, STEEPLES, HOLY WATER, BELLS, OBELISKS, WREATHS, CANDLES,

AND MORE

ORIGINATE IN

PAGAN

RELIGION.

READ
DEUT. 12

⇐ KIPA

HOLD IT . . .
IS THAT A DOME?

YES! AND I
HEAR BELLS
RINGING!

DAGON
FISH
HATS

FROM
PAGAN
ORIGINS

special hats so they could be easily distinguished from Catholics. The Catholics themselves gradually embraced the habit, so today the "clergy" wears the same headwear as you can see in the photo below.

Another odd fact: They won't even let you enter the area of the Western Wall without putting a dome (kipa) on your head. Now, picture this in your mind: let's say you're the Creator, looking at the Temple Mount area. You see hundreds of your people (Israel) facing the Western Wall *bobbing toward it.* Each one has a little dome on their head, and they are bobbing in the direction of a huge GOLD DOME on the level above them. In effect, little domes are bobbing toward the biggest dome of all. Ethnology experts have ob-

This is a photo of Bush's right hand on the Western Wall, his head domed. He and everyone else is facing EAST, talking to their Creator, right? Many BOW to this wall, and rock their bodies in its direction . . .

Four Domed Heads Try To Reconcile The Hybrid Differences

Various hats of the past

FEZ

Mandarin hat

Chinese
Thinking Cap.

Phrygian Cap

New Pope wearing Santa hat

*These photos show
Bob Dylan, Karol Wojtyla, Michael Jackson,
and the actor Gene Wilder
(from the Frisco Kid).*

Kipa on Bob Dylan

KIPA ON
MICHAEL
JACKSON

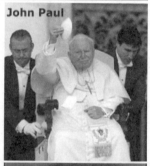

John Paul

served that the old cultures that practice witchcraft place great emphasis on the headwear of their shamans, who also often wear aprons.

EYE SERVICE — When we do something or wear something that we feel will get the attention of others, it reveals quite a bit about us. Do you imagine the gentlemen pictured on these pages were posing for a camera?   Sure, yet bet.

"Watch out for false prophets. They come to you in sheep's clothing , but inwardly they are ferocious wolves. By their fruit you will recognize them." Matt 7:15-16

From an Email:
Question: I was wondering about your position concerning women wearing tsitsith.

Answer: We promote obedience for all -- there is neither male nor female, Gentile or Yahudi, but all are **one body** (Israel). If we begin to differentiate who has to obey certain things, we have to separate into more than one body.   At least the tsitsith are found in the Torah; there are many other things forced on people that aren't.   The tsitsith were "lengthened" by some wearers in order to draw attention to them; and Yahushua called the wearers "hypocrites", which means ACTORS.   He knows our motives, He discerns our hearts and minds (Hebrews 4). On the topic of "one body", we sometimes hear teachers say that the "Jewish" believers in Messiah keep the 7th-day Shabbat, and it's not a problem at all. But then they turn and say that "Gentile" converts, or those raised as "Christians" don't have to do this.   Huh?   If we are believers in Messiah, then we obey Him.   There's no way that we are even "Gentile" any longer, but are **citizens of the commonwealth of Israel**.   There's only *ONE* body, not two.   No dividing walls, please. We know they built the wall again, and is based on what is called "replacement theology".

"And why do you worry about clothes? See how the lilies of the field grow. They do not labor or spin.   Yet I tell you that not even Solomon in all his splendor was dressed like one of these.   If that is how Elohim clothes the grass of the field, which is here today and tomorrow is thrown into the fire, will He not much more clothe you, O you of little faith?   So do not worry, saying, 'What shall we eat?' or 'What shall we drink?' or 'What shall we wear?'   For the Pagans run after all these things, and your heavenly Father knows that you need them.   But seek first His kingdom and His righteousness, and all these things will be given to you as well." Matt 6:28-33

Natsarim & *Nazirite* ARE THESE RELATED WORDS?

Natsar & Nazir -- A Crash Study of two Hebrew word roots

nazir = nun, zayin, yod, resh
natsar = nun, Tsadee, resh.

THE WORD *"NATSAR"*

There is usually some initial confusion with the words Natsar and Nazir. The original Hebrew for "Nazarene" is based on the root *"natsar"*, and means *to watch* -- this is because the area around the burg **Natsareth** was named for it, hence the word *"Gennetsaret"* (vale of Netsar) -- referring to the whole district. This root word points to the fact that the town was situated on high ground, and provided a panoramic *view* of the surroundings. It was an absolutely lovely place to grow up. The "brow of the hill" which Yahushua's townfolk tried to throw Him over gave the name to the town itself. **Natsareth** (natsar, the root) hence means *"watchtower"*, and Natsarenes are by extension "watchmen", but this also fulfills the prophecies of Yesh Yahu 11:1, Yerme Yahu 31:6, and Zec. 6:12. In these places, the change in vowels forms the root "netser", meaning "branch"; it's a kind of synonym, like any word with two meanings, but the same spelling.
"He shall be called a Natsarene" (Mt. 2:23) refers to the verses above, but it is not a direct quote as we are led to believe. This synonym (word spelled the same) forms a play-on-words: "netser", meaning "branch", and "natsar", meaning "to watch". So, we can be called branches, and watchmen for this reason. Remember Yahushua said, *"I am the vine, you are the branches"* (Yahuchanon 15:5).

The original followers of Yahushua were known as "Natsarim" (the plural of Natsari), because you'll see *"sect of the Nazarenes"* written in your translations at Acts 24:5. At Acts 28:22, we see that this "sect" was spoken against everywhere: *"And we think it right to hear from you what you think, for indeed, concerning this sect, we know that it is spoken against everywhere."* <u>*What*</u> sect?   The sect of the **Natsarim**.   The definition of "sect" is the <u>*same*</u> as the word "cult", and a "cult" is not necessarily a bad thing at all- it's only a label flung about to judge a group before thoroughly examining its teachings.   The **Natsarim** were the ORIGINAL disciples and followers of Yahushua, before Catholicism and Christianity ever existed.   The brain-washing of the masses would have us believe that Abraham was a Catholic, Muslim, or Mason;   but we know now that Kepha (Peter) wasn't a Catholic.   It would be ridiculous to think so.   Yet, Catholics believe Kepha was the "first Pope".

To believe so is an incredibly absurd conclusion.

From chapter 31 of Yerme Yahu (Jeremiah) where the promised New Covenant is located, there are the words, ***"There will be a day when WATCHMEN will cry out on the hills of Ephraim"***   (31:6) -- referring to one of the 10 lost tribes whom Yahushua was sent to, among these, some are ***"Natsarim"*** (like you and me);   and He is finishing that mission through His Natsarim today.   The word "watchmen" is from the same root, Natsar, from which we derive the words Natsareth, Gennetsaret, and Natsarim.   Technically, we should ***not*** use a letter "z" in "Nazarene", because the letter is a tsadee, or ***"ts"*** sound -- and it confuses the word with nazir, which uses a zayin (z).   A specialist in researching the historical setting of the Natsarim, brother Norman Willis expresses it the best as he says:

"The Catholic Church Father Epiphanius lived and wrote in the fourth century CE, some three hundred years after the Messiah. Epiphanius was one of the key players responsible for the establishment of the official Roman Catholic Church dogma.

In his doctrinal book, '<u>*Against* Heresies</u>,' Epiphanius wrote:
"The Nazarenes do not differ in any essential thing from them [meaning the Orthodox Jews], since they practice the customs and doctrines prescribed by Jewish Law; except that they believe in Christ.... "They believe in the resurrection of the dead, and that the universe was created by God. They preach that God is One, and that Jesus Christ is his Son.... "They are very learned in the Hebrew language. "They read the Law [meaning the Law of Moses].... "Therefore they differ...from the TRUE Christians because they fulfill until now

'Jewish' rites as the circumcision, Sabbath, and others."
[The Church Father Epiphanius in his doctrinal book, "Against Heresies," Panarion 29, 7, Page 41, 402]

Epiphanius tells us that the Nazarenes differed from what he called the "True Christians...." because they continued to fulfill "until now" such "Jewish" rites as the circumcision, the Sabbath, and others. Since Epiphanius lived and wrote in the fourth century, three hundred years after the Messiah, the Nazarenes and the Christians could only have been two Separate Groups at that time.
The Next quotation is by a modern-day Catholic Christian professor named Marcel Simon. Marcel Simon lived and worked in twentieth Century France, and he was widely regarded as being one of the leading experts on the First Century Assembly.

In his book 'Judeo-Christianity,' Professor Simon disagreed with what Epiphanius had said regarding the Nazarenes. In an effort to correct history, the Catholic Professor Simon wrote:
"They (meaning the Nazarenes) are characterized essentially by their tenacious attachment to Jewish observances. "If they became heretics in the eyes of the Mother Church , it is simply because they remained fixed on outmoded positions." [However....] "They well represent (although Epiphanius is energetically refusing to admit it) the very direct descendants of that primitive community, of which our author knows that it was designated by the Jews, by the same name, of Nazarenes'." [French Catholic Professor and First Century Assembly expert Marcel Simon, Judéo-christianisme, pp 47-48.]

Even though he was himself a practicing Roman Catholic, Marcel Simon professed that it was not the Catholic Christians, but the Nazarenes who were the "very direct descendants of that primitive community," called the Nazarenes. By this, he means that the Nazarenes (and not the Catholics) are the direct spiritual descendants of the Apostles of the New Covenant.
The Church father Epiphanius told us that there were two dif-

ferent groups, the Christians and the Nazarenes; and now Professor Simon tells us that it was the Nazarenes who descended directly from James, John, Peter, Paul, Matthew, Andrew, Phillip, and the rest. And yet, curiously, Professor Simon agrees with Epiphanius that these Nazarenes were indeed heretics, because they continued to practice the exact same worship as the Apostles had.

In other words, Professor Simon says that the Nazarenes of the fourth century became heretics simply because they continued to practice the Faith Once Delivered to the Saints." [end of Norman Willis quote]

HOW CAN WE CALL OURSELVES "NATSARIM"?

Acts 24:5 says, *"For having found this man a plague (Shaul, or Paul), who stirs up dissension among all the Yahudim throughout the world, and a ringleader of the sect of the Natsarim."*

Acts 28:22 says, *"And we think it right to hear from you what you think, for indeed, concerning this sect, we know that it is spoken against everywhere."*

YermeYahu 31:6 tells us of a day when watchmen (Hebrew, Natsarim) will arise: *"For there shall be a day when the watchmen* (Natsarim) *cry on Mount Ephrayim* (the lost tribes sown into the nations, Amos 9:9), *'Arise, and let us go up to Tsiyon, to YHWH our Elohim.'"* Also, read Ezekiel chapter 37, and Ephesians chapter 3; it is the 'secret' of Elohim, Rev. 10:7, Ephesians 3.

Our "physical" (fleshly) origins are not important; we may look Chinese, African, or Caucasian. But, we become children of YHWH by our decision to obey Him, and this shows not only our love for Him, but also it is evidence to all around us Who we serve, and Whose children we are. When we are immersed into the Name of Yahushua, and pronounce our belief in His resurrection while trusting in His blood atonement, we become His followers, and are Natsarim. Very early, the term "Natsarim" became replaced with the Gentile term "Christians". "Jesus Christ" is a man-made fabrication; "Yahushua Mashiach" is simply the order the phrase takes, because "Mashaich" is Yahushua's title, not His "last name".

Mashiach refers to His being _anointed_, the Sovereign of Israel. Shaul and Dawid were also "Mashiach", YHWH's "anointed".

THE WORD "NAZIR" -- and the Nazirite vow

By contrast, the "vow" of the "Nazirite", is based on an ancient tradition which became an institution at Num 6:1-21. The root of the word is "nazir", having distinctly different Hebrew letters:

nazir = nun, zayin, yod, resh
natsar = nun, Tsadee, resh

The word nazir means "consecrated",
similar to the word *"qodesh", or "set-apart"*.   The oath or vow of the Nazirite was for a specific period of time, and was to be taken by anyone provided they offered the prescribed offerings at Num. 6:1-21 -- but this is going to be very difficult without the Lewitical priesthood, Temple, Altar, and so on! But, if you have a *time machine*, it's a snap.   Torah specifies how the Nazirite vow was to be made.   Yahushua gave strong advice to be careful what we say, or vow!   He recommends NOT to do it - we're accountable for our vows before YHWH. The person who had taken a Nazirite vow was set-apart to YHWH for the period specified.   So, the words "Natsar" and "Nazir" are completely dissimilar.

SAMSON and LONG HAIR

The name "Samson" is really Shimshon, #8123, from #8121, sunrise, sunset, sun, west, or daylight -- and he was a **Nazirite**, *and was so from birth* (Judges 13).   He never ate or drank anything derived from **grapes**, and NEVER cut his **hair**. The problems started for him when his hair was shorn.   He kept the secret of his strength from the Philistines.   1 Cor. 11:14 seems to state that "nature" teaches us that if a man has *long hair*, it is a shame to him.   Shaul/Paul is speaking of woman's head coverings, and different perspectives which cause DIVISIONS within the assemblies.   The confusion that results from reading what Shaul is teaching arises from differences in *cultural norms*.   It may have been "shameful" at that time and place for a man to have exceedingly lengthy hair; but it certainly is not wrong for all times and places.   Samson, an Israelite of the tribe of DAN, had very, very, long hair; and it was linked to his being a **Nazirite**.   It's OK to have long hair;   Scripture teaches us that it is wrong to intentionally bring **baldness** to our heads.   Causing division, dissension, and divorce is what is to be avoided.   Proverbs 6:19 and 16:28 show us that dissension is to be avoided.

We can become a "Natsarene" because we follow Yahushua, the **Founder of our sect**.   Paul was a member of the sect of the Pharisees, but became a Natsari also -- he still considered himself a Pharisee as well.   Except for the "adding" (leavening) of the rules of the Pharisees, and their outward showing of hypocritical righteousness through eye-service, Yahushua was very much in agreement with the general pattern of the Pharisees.

WHO WERE THE "NAZARENES"? (Natsarim)

The Natsarim (*watchmen, branches*) were the sect of followers of Yahushua ha Mashiach, of Natsarith (see Acts 24:5, where Shaul was termed "a ringleader" of this sect).   How can a person discern whether or not another person is of Elohim or not?   Very simply;   if they guard Mashiach Yahushua's Commands (Torah) - see 1 Yohanan for evidence.   Which ones?   The big Ten for starters.   A person cannot live in darkness, being a lawbreaker openly, and claim to be a believer, loving YHWH:
"He that <u>has</u> My mitzvot*, and <u>keeps</u> them, he it is that loves Me: and he who loves Me, shall be loved by My Abba, and I will love him, and will reveal Myself to him," Yochanan 14:21.

"O Elohim, you are my El; early will I seek You: my being thirsts for You, my flesh longs for You in a dry and thirsty land, where no mayim is; to see Your power and Your tiferet, so as I have seen You in the Set-Apart Place. Because your loving chesed is better than chayim, my lips shall hallel you. So I will bless You while I live: I will lift up my hands to Your Name. My being shall be satisfied as with marrow and abundance; and my mouth shall hallel you with joyful lips: When I remember You upon my bed, and meditate on You in the night watches," Tehillim / Psalms 63:1-7. Selah.

* *mitzvot* IS HEBREW FOR COMMANDMENTS

THE SEVEN SABBATHS OF THE YEAR

Israel's redemption plan: shown at Deut. 16, Lev. 23

REDEMPTION is pictured (shadowed) in the **seven annual Sabbaths**, but these were "replaced" by the Replacement Theologians that designed Catholicism/Christianity. "Replacement Theology" is generally the idea that "the Church" has **replaced Israel** as the elect/chosen of YHWH. Many things were revised to accommodate the Greco-Roman mind, so a Paganized "hybrid" system of observance developed.   Paganism was *mixed-in* with the original Natsarim faith.   The "redemption plan" of Israel as set down in Scripture consists of **7 annual Sabbaths**, and these are in addition to the weekly Sabbaths (Lev. 23, Dt. 16).   So, to rid themselves of everything associated with the *true* Israel, the councils of the Roman Catholic system *eliminated* the 7 high Sabbaths of the Hebrew / Scriptural calendar, and designed a brand-new "redemption plan" of their own: the **7 sacraments**. Students of Scripture will find there is no basis for the 7 sacraments, other than to supercede the true redemption plan modeled in the 7 annual Sabbaths.

PASSOVER   This is not a "Sabbath", but the observance of Messiah's death - a remembrance. The first lamb slain in the Garden of Eden **foreshadowed** the redemption of all mankind. The shed blood covered our original parents beneath the skin of *that* lamb. A lamb died that day instead of them, but their "*immortality*" ended, and so they died within their first 1000 years, a "day" to YHWH, Who eventually provided **HIMSELF** as a Lamb, *Who takes away the sin of the world.*

Collectively, the **7 annual Sabbaths** are an "agricultural metaphor" which point to spiritual objectives. Let's look at them now:

1st day of Matsah [*1st* annual high Sabbath]   foreshadows repentance -   Come Out Of Her My People!

7th day of Matsah [*2nd* annual high Sabbath] foreshadows Immersion in the Yam Suph; also *creation* out of waters, the Great Flood, and our Covenant Immersion act (death to sin).

Shabuoth / Pentecost [*3rd* annual high Sabbath] foreshadows Messiah's Circumcision of our heart, our Covenant Oath The Good Seed, and receiving a love for the Truth, TORAH.

Yom Teruah [*4th* annual high Sabbath] foreshadows the Last Trump of warning for all occupants of Earth hear, but to Israel a recognized *call to assemble.*

Yom Kaphar [*5th* annual high Sabbath] foreshadows the Day of National Redemption, the final choice to overcome the mind of the flesh.

1st day of Sukkoth [*6th* annual high Sabbath] foreshadows our Sojourning in tents of flesh, looking forward to being fed with living Bread from Shamayim, clothed with immortality.

8th day of Sukkoth Last Great Day [*7th* annual high Sabbath] foreshadows the **Messianic Kingdom reign.**

The agricultural cycle is used to "shadow" the redemption of YHWH's *BRIDE*, which He calls "**ISRAEL OF YHWH**". Each of the 7 annual Sabbaths conceal spiritual meanings which remain hidden from those who don't practice them, and even those who do practice them from a "fleshly" approach don't see the spiritual side of them. They are so important that the elements they portray play a part in whether or not we will enter into the world-to-come! The Mashiach is the Redeemer and active Character in them all.

PASSOVER :

The year opens with PESACH, on the 14th day of the 1st moon [spring, northern hemisphere]. We remember the protection and deliverance of all Israel as they were rescued from the "bondage" of sin (Egypt) at this time of year, by the power of our Redeemer/Deliverer, YHWH with an "outstretched arm". The "door" (Yahushua, the Redeemer) is marked in a special way, indicating how our Redeemer/Deliverer covers/atones for us by marking us as protected and selected — and our decision to obey is shown by our being "observant" of this shadow of things to come. He has knocked, and we invite Him inside our dwelling. We provide evidence of our conviction that we need Him as we acknowledge His protection and deliverance from sin -- the blood-marks on the lintel and 2 doorposts signify the _wounds_ He bore for us at this time of year, and He told us to remember Him (and His death) by the emblems of bread and wine as we observe each Passover. It is His death we are to remember by observing Passover, until He comes. The First-born of YHWH died to cover sin, while the former animal sacrifices could only remind the sinner of his sinfulness. CONVICTION OF SIN is our first step.

Without the shedding of BLOOD, there is no remission (elimination) of sin.

Now, let's look into the seven observances in more detail:

UNLEAVENED BREAD

(_MATSAH_ is the Hebrew word for unleavened bread)

Next, we prepare our "soil" — our lives are cleared as a farm field for planting, by getting out the stones, boulders, and **weeds** — clearing our lives of the "sin" by our decision to repent. "Weeds" are any undesirable forms of life that are using up the resources of our lives, such as formerly Pagan customs. The departing Israelites had _plenty_ of this sort of thing in their lives. When we remove the unleavened bread, we are seeing the "shadow" of the _spiritual action_ taking place. Avoiding leaven for seven days, we are now prepared to receive **what is to be sown**. This _seven days_ is also a reflection of the "exodus" of Israel from Mitrayim/Egypt, when _they_ ate matsah until they passed through the waters of the yam suph. Something is coming into our soil to dwell and grow there - the **TORAH** (which is the personality of the Ruach, in the Name of Yahushua).

The parable of the Sower shows how we are the different types of soil. Paul told us to **"keep the feast"** (1 Co. 5:8). The seven days also picture the human lifespan, Ps. 90:10, during which we attempt to clear out the sin, clutter, and nonsense in our lives. The **1st day of Matsah** [1st annual high Sabbath] is on the 15th of the moon, and is a day of rest, recalling the departure of Israel from ha shatan's kingdom, Egypt. Israel's departure (repentance) from Satan's rule is the keynote of this day. The **7th day of Matsah** [2nd annual high Sabbath] is also a High Shabbath, and corresponds to Israel crossing the yam suph (sea of reeds) on dry ground, when Pharaoh and his army was drowned. It also relates to our immersion/baptism, as did the flood of Noach's day. As Israel obeyed YHWH to go forward, they **went into the waters**; and this is also the *beginning of our salvation by faith* (1 Pet. 3:15-22). REPENTANCE (turning around) was the *first step* away from sin, and immersion is our *second step*. During this 7-day period, we observe the **"wave sheaf offering"**, remembering the **resurrection of Yahushua**, Who is our High Priest, who was dead as our Passover Lamb, but then raised to immortality. This foreshadows the redemption of *our* bodies, since the first fruits have been waved (Yahushua's resurrection), looking forward to a great harvest of mankind later.

SHABUOTH / PENTECOST

(3rd annual high Sabbath, the *wedding anniversary*)

"Shabua" means "*week*" in Hebrew, and "Shabuoth" means "*weeks*". **Shabuoth** is the **morrow after the 7th Sabbath**, counted from the weekly Sabbath during the Feast of Matsah. Having cleared our field and made ourselves ready for the **good seed**, WE ARE PLANTED with the "good seed" of the **TORAH** at Shabuoth. Mt. Sinai was an event: the **marriage** between YHWH & ISRAEL. The "good seed" is the personality of YHWH, His Torah. These teachings are the 10 Commandments, the *wife's wedding vows*.

"When Mosheh went and told the people all Yahuah's words and laws, they responded with one voice, 'Everything Yahuah has said we will do.' Mosheh then wrote down everything Yahuah had said." Ex 24:3-4

The **bride** was saying **"I DO"** to her husband. These teachings (the TORAH Covenant) grow in us during the growing season, summer. At this time of each year we remember the giving of the Ten Commandments at Sinai in Midian, but now (in the New Covenant) they are **written on the HEARTS and MINDS of YHWH's Bride** by the indwelling Spirit of Yahushua, Who circumcises His Commandments into us so we LOVE the Covenant. It's our wedding anniversary. The same 10 Commands given in stone are now written on our tablets of flesh, fulfilling the "NEW" (or re-newed) Covenant promised at Yerme Yahu 31:31-34, Ezek. 36:26,27; Yerme Yahu 31 is quoted at Heb. Chapters 8 & 10. Our immersion pictures our circumcision, as a Bride washes after her period of unclean-ness, when we make our *personal* COVENANT with Ya-hushua to obey Him as a Bride obeys a Husband. The first Natsarim received the Spirit of Yahushua *at this time* — We are His Temple now.   The "Ark" of the Covenant was just a box made of gold — but we are so much more than it was. We contain the living Elohim, Maker of Heavens and Earth, *and His Personality* (the Torah) *grows into our being as we practice obeying His Commandments* — this is evidence that we are His (1 John 2:3-6).   The third step is obedience, and begins with our immersion, **accepting the Covenant** (10 Commandments), and going to the water as our outward sign of becoming Yahushua's Bride, *joining Israel*, escaping the spirit of the world (mind of the flesh).   Accepting the Cove-nant by immersion, *we become Israel* and His *wife*; we agree to obey our Husband, and He CIRCUMCISES our hearts with the Covenant, allowing us to LOVE the Torah, the Ten Com-mandments.   "Sinai" happens to us personally, and our im-mersion is our circumcision by the Spirit of Yahushua in our hearts, the objective being love, evidenced by our obedience.

THE SEVENTH MONTH

A final warning comes at the beginning of the seventh moon.   (The Hebrew word "YOM" simply means day).
Yom Teruah [4th annual high Sabbath] is a day for the blow-ing of a shofar, pre-shadowing the "last trump".   "Yom" means day, and "Teruah" means shout, as with a shofar. This is observed on the 1st day of the 7th moon.

Yom Kaphar (known as Yom Kippur) "DAY OF COVERING"

On the 10th day of the seventh moon we are JUDGED at **Yom Kaphar** [5th annual high Sabbath] (the 10th day of the seventh month, called **"the Fast"** at Acts 27:9). The Judge of all flesh will one day look at each person, and decide whether or not they are of the wheat or the weeds, and **separate them** as with a winnowing fork.

Sukkoth or Tabarnacles, Tents

Some day, we will be HARVESTED (the feast of the har-vest, called Tabernacles, or SUKKOT).   The **final** two high Sabbaths are the **1st day of Sukkoth** [6th annual high Sab-bath], and the **8th day of Sukkoth** [7th annual high Sabbath], the last great day closing the festival.   TABERNACLES:

Yahushua was born in the fall, during the commanded feast of YHWH called "SUKKOTH", meaning tents or booths (Tabernacles) see Lev. 23, Dt. 16. He was visited by the shepherds (but not the Magi) on the night of His birth, and these shepherds were told He could be found lying in a feeding trough (Luke 2).

Similar to the hut our Messiah was born in, we are told to build a temporary dwelling and place branches freshly cut from trees of the brook upon it. This very clearly "shadows" our own bodies, our "tent". The seventy years of our life are pictured by the **seven days**, and we notice the branches slowly whither and die over the seven days of this feast. The Messiah of Israel was born during the Feast of Sukkot, most likely on the 1st day. He was circumcised in His flesh on the 7th day - marking the two High Sabbaths of Sukkoth.

Last Great Day

The day following Sukkoth we have the day named **"Simchat Torah"**, meaning "rejoicing with the Torah". The primary thing about this day is JOY. It foreshadows the world-to-come, the millennial reign of our Messiah, when Israel's **redemption** is completely fulfilled. We are clothed with immortality, and enter into the New Yerushalyim.

Redemption is foreshadowed in the observances that were taken from us by the wiles of the devil, but we have overcome by the blood of Yahushua. We get it now. The "cup" filled with the abominations and the filthiness of the whoring of Babel the Great, imposed on us through Catholicism and her daughters, is fallen. You can read of this at Rev. 17 & 18.

These "shadows" of things-to-come will be understood better by practicing them. For now, we should observe the "times" appointed for us, and be mindful that it is not in the details of how "perfectly" we perform them, or of being critical of others as they observe them. Rather, we must understand what these "shadows" represent spiritually, and grow in our appreciation and love for YHWH — and love for those He has redeemed. As imperfect as we all are in our various levels of development, we are all very special to Him. We not only are commanded to love one another, but also our enemies. We are the living TEMPLE of YHWH, and living waters (the TO-

RAH) should flow from each of us. Remember to forgive, because no one is perfect except One: Yahushua ha Mashiach L'Natsareth. Those of the synagogue of Satan must leave it and begin to *restore what has been lost*, and return to their First Love: TORAH. You can live in the "Torah Zone" now, by observing the Commandments of Yahuah. Your family and friends will make you feel like you're in the "Twilight Zone", but that's to be expected. The **Living Word** (Debar Chayim, Yahushua' Spirit) is living and active; it is a double-edged Sword, and able to discern between soul and spirit, joints and marrow, and to judge the thoughts and intentions of the heart (see Hebrews 4). Everything you see is passing away, but everything you cannot see is eternal. The **Torah** is the only thing you can take with you from this lifetime, and if you don't have it now, ask Yahushua and He will give it to you. It is "living water", and drinking from it you will never thirst.

"And He showed me a river of water of life (mayim chayim)*, clear as crystal, coming from the Throne of Elohim and of the Lamb. In the middle of its street, and on either side of the river, was the tree of life* (ets chayim)*, which bore twelve fruits, each tree yielding its fruit every month. And the leaves of the tree were for the healing of the nations.* Rev. 22:1.2

Israel is the beloved of Yahuah, and to *become* Israel all we must do is observe Yahuah's Covenant (Yesha Yahu 56). To remove ourselves, all we have to do is *stop observing* Yahuah's Covenant. We don't need anyone's "permission" to believe and obey. We are either in the Torah Zone, or we're not. Israel's highest duty is to love Yahuah, and love their "neighbor". *"Doing Yahuah's Commands"* involve these two essential things predicated on LOVE.

"Blessed are those doing His Commands, so that the authority shall be theirs unto the tree of life, and to enter through the gates into the city. But outside are the dogs and those who enchant with drugs, and those who whore, and the murderers, and the idolaters, and all who love and do falsehood." Rev. 22:14

Israel has the Living Water, the **Torah** of **Yahuah**. Famine and drought result from the lack of it - and that's death.

The true worship of Yahuah, His Torah, has been laid waste by the "abominations" of Babel the Great, but he that overcomes will drink of the *water of life*, the Torah.

"It is done. I am the Alef and the Tau, the Beginning and the End. To him who is thirsty I will give to drink without cost from the spring of the <u>water</u> of <u>life</u>. He who <u>overcomes</u> will inherit all this, and I will be his Elohim and he will be my son. But the cowardly, the unbelieving, the vile, the murderers, the sexually immoral, those who practice magic arts, the idolaters and all liars—their place will be in the fiery lake of burning sulfur. This is the second death." Rev 21:6-8

We cannot possibly believe for a moment that men hold the reigns of deciding who receives eternal life and who doesn't. And yet, there are men who claim they do. The only true "saints" *(qodeshim)* are Israel, and they are walking around us every day. We call ourselves "Natsarim" because we follow **Yahushua of Natsarith**, trust in His atoning death, and have eternal life because He is resurrected and lives in us. To the Mother of Harlots, we are heretics. To the Islamic, we are infidels because we don't believe that Muhammad is the Prophet. To the worldly evolutionists, we are mentally ill and need to be either "cured" or put out of our misery. Yet, when a little while passes, these will not be found. We are going to inherit the Earth, and we will not have to conquer anyone with hate, but love. Living in the "Torah Zone", hatred is not known.

Thank you for wrestling with these topics along with me.

*Remember,
one of the meanings of
"Yisra'el" is*

He who wrestles with El

*Author,
Lew White*

It's only a realm of love, ruled by the Eternal One,
the Ancient of Days,

Yahushua, the King of kings

OTHER ARTICLES

If you are looking for other articles written by this author, they can be found on the web site:

www.fossilizedcustoms.com

Two other books by this author are also available:

Fossilized Customs -
The Pagan Sources of Popular Customs

In The Twinkling Of An Eye - *The End Of Days*

Call 502-261-9833 or visit the web site for ordering details.

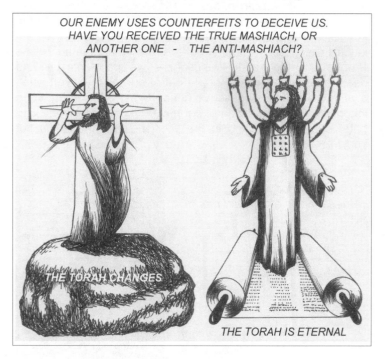

"He that dwells in the secret place of the Most High shall abide under the shadow of the Almighty. I will say of ㆐Y㆐Ɫ, He is my refuge and my fortress: my Elohim; In Him will I trust.

"Surely He shall deliver you from the trap of the hunter, and from the destructive pestilence. He shall cover you with His feathers, and under His wings shall you trust: His emet shall be your shield and armor.

"You shall not be afraid for the terror by night; nor of the arrow that flies by day, nor for the pestilence that walks in darkness; nor for the destruction that ravages at noonday.

"A thousand shall fall at your side, and ten thousand at your right hand; but it shall not come near you.

"Only with your eyes shall you observe and see the reward of the wicked. Because you have made ㆐Y㆐Ɫ, Who is my refuge, even the Most High, your dwelling place;

"There shall no evil befall you, neither shall any plague come near your dwelling, For He shall give His heavenly messengers charge over you, to keep you in all your halachot. They shall bear you up in their hands, lest you dash your foot against a stone.

"You shall trample upon the lion and cobra; the young lion and the serpent shall you trample under feet. Because he has set his ahava upon Me, therefore will I deliver him: I will set him on high, because he has known My Name. He shall call upon Me, and I will answer him: I will be with him in trouble; I will deliver him, and honor him. With long chayim will I satisfy him, and show Him My Yahshua." Tehillim - Psalms 91

EMET: TRUTH (WORD, TORAH)   HALACHOT: WAYS   AHAVA: LOVE

CREDIT CARD ORDERS BY PHONE: 502-261-9833 (fax: 502-297-9854)

NEED IT FAST?

THE SCRIPTURES ISBN: 0-620-22490-8

HARD COVER, *RESTORES THE NAME OF OUR CREATOR TO THE TEXT IN EACH PLACE IT OC-CURS IN THE INSPIRED HEBREW.* THIS NEW VERSION IN ENGLISH IS A LITERAL TRANSLATION OF GENESIS THROUGH REVELATION, AND USES THE "MODERN" HEBREW LETTERS FOR THE NAME: [YHWH: hvhy YAHUSHUA: iwvhy] HARD COVER $33.00; **Soft Cover Editions: $23**
LEATHER EDITION — 6" X 9" : GOLD LEAF EDGES, $76.00 EACH.

FOSSILIZED CUSTOMS (ILLUSTRATED) ISBN: 0-9584353-6-7

(184 pgs) BY LEW WHITE; A MESSIANIC ISRAELITE BOOK EXPLAINING THE PAGAN ORIGINS OF CHRISTMAS, EASTER, SUN-DAY, THE CALENDAR, AND MUCH MORE. A UNIQUE OUTREACH TOOL THAT WILL ANSWER QUESTIONS YOU HAVEN'T EVEN THOUGHT TO ASK! IF YOU'D LIKE TO HAND SOMEONE SOMETHING (IN ADDITION TO THE SCRIPTURES) THAT CONTAINS EVERYTHING YOU'D LIKE TO TELL THEM, THIS WOULD BE THE BOOK.
   1 COPY: $9.95 — 4 COPIES: $20.00 — 10 OR MORE COPIES: $3.00 EACH
   BECOME A DISTRIBUTOR OF FC AUTOMATICALLY WITH ANY ORDER OF 10 OR MORE

IN THE TWINKLING OF AN EYE - THE END OF DAYS

(116 pgs) BY LEW WHITE; IS THE RAPTURE FOR REAL? WHO ARE THE ELECT? THIS BOOK DISCUSSES THE TWO WITNESSES, THE TRIBULATION, AN OVERVIEW OF THE FALL AND RE-DEMPTION, AND THE POSSIBILITY THAT ONE OF THE ORIGINAL APOSTLES *IS STILL ALIVE TO-DAY.* IN THIS BOOK THE **SECRET OF ELOHIM** IS REVEALED, FROM SCRIPTURE.
   1 COPY: $7.95 - 5 COPIES: $20.00 - 10 OR MORE COPIES: $3.00 EACH

COME OUT OF HER MY PEOPLE ISBN: 0-620-20144-4

(160 pgs) BY CHRIS KOSTER; A COMPANION BOOK WITH FOSSILIZED CUSTOMS. WELL DOCU-MENTED, IT PROVIDES THE READER WITH DETAILED ETYMOLOGY, AND SHOWS HOW CHRISTI-ANITY BECAME PAGANIZED, EMBRACING THE GENTILE CUSTOMS OF SUN WORSHIP FROM BABY-LON. **1 COPY: $12.95; - 10 COPIES: $80.00**

VIRUS FIGHTER: **SAMBUCOL LOZENGES** (30) $12.95

FIGHTS FLU, COLD, HERPES; MADE KOSHER IN JERUSALEM, ISRAEL, FROM BLACK ELDERBERRY

CANCER FIGHTER: **FLOR-ESSENCE** (DRY, MAKES 3 QTS) $29.95

8-HERB "TEA", ATTACKS ONLY THE CANCER — COMES WITH RE-USEABLE BREWING BAG

VITAMINS: **NATURE'S PLUS** (90 TABLETS) WORLD'S BEST! $29.95

MULTI-VITAMIN & MINERAL SUPPLEMENT (HELP CELLS NOT MAKE "COPY ERRORS")

SHIRTS: L, XL WITH NAME " ayaz " IN WHITE LETTERING $15.00

HEAVY T-SHIRT, ROYAL BLUE, WITH 3/4" LETTERS IMPRINTED ON LEFT FRONT BREAST

HEBREW CALENDARS Runs from Sept. to Sept. 10" X 18"

shows new moons and the feast days according to orthodox interpretation of Torah

   SPIRAL BOUND A GREAT GUIDE TO HAVE TO CALCULATE MO'EDIM
   ALSO CONTAINS SCRIPTURE LOCATIONS FOR STUDYING TORAH PORTIONS
NORMALLY ONLY AVAILABLE BETWEEN "MAY" TO "JAN" *$8.95 or 2 for $12*

INTERNATIONAL ORDERS - INTERNATIONAL MONEY ORDERS OR BANK CARDS ONLY - ADD 45% S&H